Finding Faith

Finding Faith

In the City Care Forgot

WRITTEN BY TEENA MYERS

TATE PUBLISHING
AND ENTERPRISES, LLC

Finding Faith in the City Care Forgot
Copyright © 2012 by Teena Myers. All rights reserved.

No part of this publication may be reproduced, stored in a retrieval system or transmitted in any way by any means, electronic, mechanical, photocopy, recording or otherwise without the prior permission of the author except as provided by USA copyright law.

All scripture quotations, unless otherwise indicated, are taken from the *Holy Bible, New International Version*®, niv®. Copyright ©1973, 1978, 1984 by Biblica, Inc.™ Used by permission of Zondervan. All rights reserved worldwide. www.zondervan.com

Scripture quotations marked (kjv) are taken from the *Holy Bible, King James Version*, Cambridge, 1769. Used by permission. All rights reserved.

The opinions expressed by the author are not necessarily those of Tate Publishing, LLC.

This book is designed to provide accurate and authoritative information with regard to the subject matter covered. This information is given with the understanding that neither the author nor Tate Publishing, LLC is engaged in rendering legal, professional advice. Since the details of your situation are fact dependent, you should additionally seek the services of a competent professional.

Published by Tate Publishing & Enterprises, LLC
127 E. Trade Center Terrace | Mustang, Oklahoma 73064 USA
1.888.361.9473 | www.tatepublishing.com

Tate Publishing is committed to excellence in the publishing industry. The company reflects the philosophy established by the founders, based on Psalm 68:11,
"The Lord gave the word and great was the company of those who published it."

Book design copyright © 2012 by Tate Publishing, LLC. All rights reserved.
Cover design by Brandon Land
Interior design by Christina Hicks
Author photo taken and provided by Cyndi McMurray

Published in the United States of America

ISBN: 978-1-61862-686-8
1. Religion / Christian Life / Inspirational
2. Religion / Christian Life / General
12.08.13

To Rebecca Willman Gernon,
who gave me no rest until I turned
these stories into a book.

Table of contents

Introduction 9
In Pain but Not in Vain : Lori Landry 15
Hound of Heaven : Jeremy Quintini 19
Radically Changed : Bill Shanks 27
Tarzan of Manhattan : Jim Siracuse 35
A Love Story : Max and Carla Miller 41
A Burning Bush Experience : Jim Chester 47
Is That All There Is? : Sandy Cash 53
The Lost Boys : Slater Armstrong 59
Treasure in Cell #7 : Donald Eskine 63
From Montreal to Ottawa : Kenneth Landriault 69
The Creative Dramatist : Kathy Frady 77
She's Not in Kansas Anymore : Myrindia Warner 81
God's Family : Jeff and Jennifer Oettle 85
Three Powerful Words : Matt Degier 93
Living on the Fringe : Pamela Davis-Noland 97
Like Any Normal Day : Mark and Janice McLean . . . 103
Looking for Love : Tasha 109
Make Me Ordinary : Pam Harrelson 117
Between the First and Second Pew : Rhonda Rock . . . 123
The Star Maker : David Crosby 129
Hazard's Journey : Pat Hazard 135
Wait on the Lord : Joe McKeever 141
A Ray of Hope : Milena Rimassa 147
Trusting God : Robert Comeaux 153
He Brought Peace : Michelle Beadle 157
Engulfed in Fire : Wade Moody 165

A Spiritual Gift : Anthony Freeman. 175
Prodigal Daughter : Christa Allan. 181
A Lot from a Little : Cissy Padgett 187
It's Not What You Can Do : George Zanca. 193
God's Gift to the Ninth Ward : Robert Burnside 201
A Shiny Pebble : Kathy Baker. 207
Never Too Old : Betty Burke 215
Faith, Trust, and Reason : Pamela Binnings Ewen. . . . 219
Fit for Service : Elizabeth Garcia-Smith 227
God's Shepherds : Thomas and Tawanna Gross. 233
He Hasn't Failed Me Yet : Ellen Brown. 241
Devils Beware : Janyce Stratton 245
Who Is Anna Donahue? : Anna Donahue. 255
Miracle at St. Rita's : James Jeffries 261
Thank You : David Rodriguez. 267
Friends : Anthony Marquize. 275
The Communications Guy : Paul Malinich 281
Atheist Said : David Brown 285
Conclusion. 301
About the Author 303

Introduction

I sat beside Emma, a former student from my defunct Bible study class, listening to church announcements. She slipped an offering envelope into my hand. Perplexed, I looked at the envelope and said, "Do you want me to put it in the offering basket?"

"No," said Emma. "It's for your ministry."

"What ministry?"

"Your writing ministry," she replied.

I shoved the envelope back into Emma's hand. "Put that in the offering basket. I don't have a ministry."

She shoved the envelope into my hand. "No, it's for you."

I raised the envelope to eye level and jabbed the church name with my finger. "It's not for me. It's for the church. See the name on the envelope?" I shoved the envelope into her hand.

Emma glared at me and tried to shove the envelope into my hand now formed into a tight fist.

"I'm not taking money in a church's offering envelope," I whispered through clenched teeth.

Emma ripped open the envelope, dropped the cash onto my lap, and said, "It's for your ministry."

The look in her eye threatened physical altercation if I dared give the money back. Lest we start a World Wrestling Federation Smack Down in the middle of a church service, I put the cash in my Bible and said, "Fine."

Thus began my journey to publishing, but I had some problems. First, if I had known God wanted me to write, I would have paid attention in English class. My grammar was atrocious. Second, I didn't know how to write whatever I was supposed to write. A collection of lessons written for my Sunday school class became my first very messy, unmarketable failure.

Rod, my husband, was more interested in my writing activities than I was. He mentioned I should join a writing group. People of like minds reading each other's work to offer advice for improvement intrigued me. I scoured the Internet for a local group. Nothing. I tried the newspaper. Nothing. In the events column, the library was offering a class about writing. I jotted down the date and time and went to the class, expecting nothing.

At the conclusion of the meeting, one of the attendees announced a writer's critique group met weekly in a local bookstore. Jackpot! The following Monday, I walked into the bookstore and wandered about the two-story building until I found three people sitting at a table near the bathroom. I claimed an empty seat at the table. They were fiction writers. I wrote nonfiction and assumed that I was attending my first and last meeting. When they learned I was published, the leader of the group made an exception. Even though he envisioned a single genre of writers, his ultimate purpose for the group was to encourage the craft of writing, so he swung the door open for all genres.

The group consisted of a sci-fi writer who thought God created injustice, a Lutheran humor writer, and a Pagan who wrote historical fiction. Eventually, an agnostic attorney writing an epic, a Jew who wrote intrigue, and an atheist fiction writer joined. Many others came and left when they learned they would not be depositing a million dollar advance check any time soon, perhaps never.

This eclectic group of writers taught me how to write and eventually guided me to toward my purpose. During my time with them, I set aside the Bible lessons and dabbled in fiction. My first fiction short story became a bestseller on Amazon.com's Shorts program when there were only nine religion entries. Amazon was not obligated to mail a royalty check under $25, and I never saw a penny from that now abandoned program. But the experience changed my nonfiction style of writing to include dialogue, preparing me for my next destination.

Several years after I joined the critique group, a friend told me about the Southern Christian Writers Guild. Shortly after I joined, Milena Rimassa, the Northshore Bureau Chief for NOLA.com, shared her writing experiences. At the conclusion of her presentation, she extended an invitation to submit articles for a new blog called Faith, Beliefs, and Spirituality. Milena had envisioned a community of writers posting articles to the blog. She got me.

At the time, I was co-writing skits with a friend for my drama team. Thinking I would be one of many writers making contributions, I planned to upload videos of the drama team's performances and post an occasional devotion. "In his heart a man [in my case, a woman] plans his course, but the Lord determines his steps" (Proverbs 16:9). Instead of uploading videos, I found myself navigating the narrow one-way streets of New Orleans, traveling down the longest bridge in America and getting lost in the bayous of south Louisiana as I pursued stories of faith.

My sister's long struggle with drug abuse became my first written contribution to the faith blog and the first chapter of this book. Even though Lori and I had attended the same church, she never found the freedom that I did. Her struggle taught me a valuable lesson. Then I floundered looking for bearings: a devotion, news about church events, testimonies of answered prayers.

I found my stride the day popular Bible teacher Anna Donahue repeatedly came to my attention. She became the subject of my first profile, *Who is Anna Donahue?* I outlined her journey from broadcasting news to broadcasting the love of God. An unshakable name occurred more than once. Pastor Anthony Marquize, who was running for the United States House of Representatives, came to my attention three times in one day. I already had a list of people waiting for me to write their story and opted not to contact him. Before the week ended, I met him at a minister's fellowship and relented. His story left me in awe. He lost the election but gained something greater. Finally, I denied multiple invitations to Dr. Kathy Baker's Interfaith Bible study before a friend convinced me to attend. Dr. Baker's story, *A Shiny Pebble*, gave me more than fodder for a book. She became a cherished friend.

Friends were a rich resource of remarkable stories. Jeremy Quintini, a lively child in my husband's children service, fulfilled a 100-year-old prophecy in a foreign nation. Pamela Binnings Ewen's struggle to find a faith compatible with reason produced credible evidence that the gospel stories can be trusted. George Zanca disqualified himself from pastoral ministry, but God did not. Mark McLean stared out his office window in the World Financial Center at the aftermath of the first plane's collision with the Twin Towers. He looked up to witness the second plane heading for his office.

I entertained the idea of compiling the stories into a book in response to an atheist's challenge. "Teena, I don't care what God did thousands of years ago in the lives of shepherds. Tell me what God is doing today," he said. The idea sat simmering on the back burner for a long time. I was busy and planned to do it another day. That day came when friend and fellow writer Rebecca Gernon nagged me into presenting the idea to an agent at a writer's conference. The agent's interest was unexpected. His request to see the manuscript forced me to write one. He later declined the project, and I laid my rejected work at God's feet. "If you want this to be published," I prayed, "give me a publisher." Obviously, he did.

Ironically, the atheist with a challenge, one of the nicest people I know, solidified my faith in God. I sat in a café sipping coffee as David Brown preached the atheist's gospel to me. His gospel sounded identical to mine except for the rock we embraced. "Atheist Said" is among my favorites and the last chapter in this book.

Another favorite is "Thank You." My conversation with Pastor David Rodriguez solved a thirty-eight-year-old mystery.

Do you wonder if God still intervenes in human lives? Does he still answer prayer and fulfill prophecy? Can he heal us spiritually, mentally, and physically? Will he give us hope, direction, peace, protection, and encouragement? Read the evidence in this book and decide for yourself.

In Pain but Not in Vain

In a drug-induced stupor, Lori sat in the bathtub, turned on the hot water, and passed out. My mother found her in a tub of scalding water with fifty percent of her body severely burned. After six months in a coma, an infection destroyed her vital organs. The death certificate said "renal failure." My sister died as she had lived—in pain but not in vain.

When we were children, Lori walked to a Baptist church. She later told me that she did so for the cookies and juice. After our family moved to New Orleans, we were swept into the local drug culture. When I converted to Christianity, Lori followed me to church. Our father didn't understand our zeal for God and spat with disgust. "I'd rather have a daughter on drugs than involved in this Jesus stuff." Lori fulfilled his desire and returned to the immediate gratification drugs offered. To our father's distress, she did whatever she pleased until her unrestrained lifestyle resulted in her incarceration.

I thought God had given up on Lori, but I was wrong. Shortly after she was released from prison, she obtained a respectable job in a hospital. How could that happen without divine intervention? Lori mastered her craft and received letters of accolades from her employers. She gave birth to a beautiful daughter and lived to give her only child the best she could afford. She even returned to church.

God had not given up on Lori, but she had built her house on shifting sands. She served God as many immature Christians do: to obtain what they desire. Lori desired God to release the man she loved from a life sentence in prison. After ten years of believing for a miracle, Lori lost hope. She interpreted an unfulfilled desire as "God doesn't love me" and abandoned the church.

I thought God gave up on her, but I was wrong. He spared her from drug overdoses. "Another thirty seconds and I could not have brought her back," the emergency room doctor said to me.

Friends had abandoned her at the door of the emergency room thinking she was dead. Tears filled my eyes as I looked at my sister's emaciated body lying on a hospital bed. She opened her eyes.

"I wish he would have let me die," she moaned.

Lori survived numerous automobile accidents. She drove her car into the bedroom of a house. Fortunately, the bed was not occupied that night. She walked away unharmed. Two people died in another wreck. She lived. She drove her car into another house. The homeowner dragged her from the car seconds before a broken gas line caused an explosion. Death knocked at her door so many times; she acknowledged only God could be keeping her alive. Lori thought God repeatedly spared her life because he loved me. She couldn't have been more wrong.

God returned her to a place of sanity, and a college hired her to be my husband's secretary. How does someone with an eighth-grade education survive the scrutiny of PhDs without divine intervention? I marveled at the depth of God's love, but what had become clear to me, Lori could not see. God loved Lori.

A path littered with wounded people struggling to forgive you makes it difficult to find your way home. When Lori showed signs that old demons had returned, I thought surely God had given up on her this time. Once again, I was wrong.

Carol, a friend I love like a sister, interpreted for the deaf in the classroom next to Lori's office. From the moment they met, the urgency to pray for Lori pursued Carol twenty-four hours a day—in the middle of the night, while she was in the shower, cleaning house, driving down the highway. One morning on her way to work, Carol said, "God, if you want me to pray for Lori today, let her come out of her office to drink a cup of coffee, or smoke a cigarette, or go to the bathroom." When Carol pulled into the parking lot, Lori came out of her office holding a cup of coffee, lit up a cigarette, and was on her way to the bathroom.

Lori slipped into depression as her addiction returned. She lost her job at the college, checked herself into a psych ward, and emerged to be hired by a doctor. The doctor offered her more money than she requested with promise of a generous increase after initial training. Everyone on his staff was a Christian. Lori had every reason to be encouraged.

She called me frequently. We talked about God. She talked about regrets and mistakes. She longed for the days when she went to church on Sunday and intercessory prayer on Monday. I invited Lori to spend the weekend with me and witnessed a different person. I believed she was sincere about changing her ways and hopeful she would succeed. She didn't.

Free will is a blessing or a curse perched precariously upon the choices we make. Similar to Israel in the wilderness, Lori and I ate the same spiritual food and drank the same spiritual drink (1 Corinthians 10). I heeded the Bible's admonition to flee from sin. She enjoyed its pleasures and reaped the consequences of her choice.

For most of Lori's life, I thought God had given up on her. As I stared at her lifeless body lying serenely in a casket, I realized that he never did. Lori lived in pain but not in vain. She taught me what my finite mind could not imagine: the infinite depth of God's love.

Teena Myers

Hound of Heaven

I met Jeremy Quintini in my husband's children's church. Jeremy was one of the lively children who, allegedly, never got a snowball coupon for good behavior. His mother and I became close friends. She often shared news of Jeremy's spiritual progress as he grew into a young adult. When he traveled to Vanautu, an island in the South Pacific, as a missionary, my husband and I sent financial support. I learned we had made a good investment when I requested to write about Jeremy's ministry.

"My parents were godly," said Jeremy, "so I knew all the Christian stuff, but I just didn't get it for a long time. To me Jesus was cliché, a fiction character, like Superman. Every time your husband gave an altar call, I followed the other kids to the altar. I thought that made me a Christian. But I didn't know God, and I gave my parents a lot of trouble."

I knew Jeremy had been difficult, but his mother never revealed the detail Jeremy shared with me. "I never got drunk or took drugs, but I didn't have a greater morality than my friends. I was being pursued by the hound of heaven," said Jeremy, and then he explained that the hound of heaven was a reference to Francis Thompson's poem about God's relentless pursuit of sinful humanity.

When Jeremy was ten years old, he attended a Christian youth camp. A man asked him if he knew what *Jeremiah* meant. Before he could respond, the man said, "Jeremiah means 'called of the Lord.' He is calling you to serve him in a unique way. There are bridges in people's lives that the enemy has destroyed. The Lord will use you to rebuild those bridges." Later, an evangelist made a similar statement, but Jeremy was suspicious that the men had conspired to tell him the same thing.

"The doctors told my parents I had attention deficit disorder, but I never believed that. There was evil in me that refused to be controlled. I made my parents miserable, fought with my brother, and treated my sisters like enemies. No matter what I did, I couldn't break my mother's iron will, and the sight of my dad reading the Bible and praying every morning haunted me."

By the end of Jeremy's sophomore year of high school, he grew weary of fighting. When his sister invited him to a Christian concert, he accepted, hoping they could develop a relationship. Jeremy sat on the back row, arms folded defiantly across his chest, trying to digest the scene before him. Hundreds of kids were praying with an emotion he didn't understand until the band sang "Yahweh" by Andy Park.

"When the band sang, 'Let your goodness pass before us, right before our eyes,' I felt like I was looking at pieces of a puzzle and recognizing patterns in them, and then the pieces suddenly came together. Someone started preaching after that, but I didn't pay attention to what he said. I was stunned and wanted to go home and think."

As Jeremy and his sister were leaving the concert, a man extended his hand to Jeremy and said, "So you're finally here."

"What do you mean?" said Jeremy.

"I met you when you were twelve, and the Lord told me that I would mentor you."

For the next two years, James patiently instructed Jeremy in the practical application of spiritual truths to his life. As they studied the Bible together, Jeremy realized answering an altar call didn't impart salvation. Faith in God did. When Jeremy's contentious behavior continued, James explained the process of sanctification, easing Jeremy's frustration.

Jeremy graduated from high school and enrolled in Christ for the Nations Institute (CFNI). He immediately clicked with Jim, his roommate, whose father was the chief operations officer for Reinhard Bonnke's Christ for All Nations (CFAN) ministry.

"The school required an internship," said Jeremy. "We could work at the college for the summer or go on a mission trip. We planned a mission trip to Chile. Several of the students on our team failed to raise enough money, and the trip was canceled. That's when Jim called his dad to see if we could do an internship at CFAN."

Jeremy arrived at the Florida office of CFAN, thinking the internship would be a summer vacation. Jim's father warned them that he would work them hard. He kept his word. The boys worked a forty-hour week and spent many evenings doing yard work. Their duties included personal tasks for Reverend Bonnke.

Jeremy met the German evangelist for the first time when he picked him up at the airport. As Jeremy performed a variety of tasks at Bonnke's home, they developed a relationship, and Jeremy asked him about a much debated topic at school.

"Reverend Bonnke, what do you think about Calvinism?"

"College talk." Reverend Bonnke pounded his desk as he quoted 2 Peter 3:9: "The Lord is not slow in keeping his promise, as some understand slowness. He is patient with you, not wanting anyone to perish, but everyone to come to repentance." The intensity of Bonnke's reply made Jeremy reluctant to argue.

"Jeremy," said Reverend Bonnke, "What do you feel the Lord is calling you to do?"

"Honestly, I don't know. I just want to see people saved."

Jeremy saw excitement in Reverend Bonnke's eyes. "This is the heart of an evangelist. The evangelist preaches the ABCs, the preliminary truths of Christianity, the XYZs for anyone else."

Bonnke's dedication to his calling amazed Jeremy. One day, Bonnke said to Jeremy, "I've been preaching the gospel for fifty years. People talk to me about retirement. Never! I will preach as long as the Lord gives me breath, and after, bury me under the pulpit."

Jeremy watched a video of one of Bonnke's crusades in Africa. To Jeremy, a million people chanting, "Bonnke, Bonnke, Bonnke," sounded like an earthquake. The next time he spoke to Reverend Bonnke, he asked, "How do you protect yourself against pride?"

Reverend Bonnke looked at Jeremy as though he had never thought about it. "Pride? What are you talking about? I've never cared about their criticism. Why should I care about their praise? Men chanting my name is like Israel praying to the God of Abraham, Isaac, and Jacob. The Africans were not chanting for me but for the God of Bonnke."

Jeremy looked at me and said, "He is the most humble man I've ever met. Everything he spoke was with thunder. One day we were in his car, and he pounded on the dash as he said, 'Faith is not merely subscribing to correct doctrines. The just shall live by their faith. Faith is doing.'"

Jeremy returned to college transformed by the summer he had spent with a Christian legend. A month before graduation, Jeremy; Mike, the assistant mission director for CFNI; and Nathan, a friend of Jeremy's, drove to a nearby lake to hit golf balls. They were talking about their future plans when Mike said, "Jeremy, I forgot to tell you a hurricane devastated the island of Vanuatu. The college is building a Bible school on the island. Would you like to go with us?"

Bonnke's statement "Faith is doing" thundered in Jeremy's thoughts. Without hesitation he said, "I'm in."

"Dude," said Nathan. "Don't you think you should pray about that?"

Jeremy looked at Nathan and spoke with the confidence of Reverend Bonnke. "No, I don't need to pray about it. I know. Let's go."

Jeremy traveled to Vanuatu, a collection of eighty-three islands, with Mike and twelve student interns.

"Everything was exciting," said Jeremy. "We landed in Port Villa and then traveled into the bush country to preach the gospel. The people spoke English, French, and Pigeon, but most of the time we communicated in English. After the students returned to America, Mike and I went to the village of Kitow on the island of Tanna to build the Bible school." Other mission groups from America soon joined them to help with the construction. Together they put a roof on the church and helped construct six buildings for the Bible school.

Once a month, people came from all over the island to attend a five-day Bible course. When Mike and Jeremy learned about a village that didn't have anyone attending the Bible school, they sent a message to its chief requesting permission to preach the gospel. The chief sent word that they couldn't come. Mike and Jeremy felt they should go, so they sent another message. The chief replied that they would be killed if they came to the village.

"Mike was ready to be a martyr, but I wasn't so sure," said Jeremy. "The chief and his son didn't want us there, but some of the villagers did, so we decided to go."

Mike and Jeremy made plans to travel to the village on Tuesday but awoke to a terrible storm. They left the following day with a team of seven people. The storm had made the trail to the village slippery. They constantly stopped to help one another as they slipped in the mud. Four hours later, they entered the village, exhausted and covered in mud. When the curious villagers gathered around the missionaries, they preached the gospel to them. To their amazement, everyone in the village accepted Christ.

The next day, the team traveled to a neighboring village that had already received word of the missionaries' success. "Do you know why the entire village received you?" the village chief asked.

"What do you mean?" said Jeremy.

"A hundred years ago, a missionary came to convert the village, but they killed him. As he lay dying, he prophesied, 'When the cane is run out and you are no longer able to build your homes, two white American missionaries will teach you how to build eternal homes and your culture will be changed.' That is why the chief and his son threatened to kill you if you preached the gospel in their village, but they died in the storm the day before you arrived. The villagers believed they had offended your God, and that is why they received your message."

Jeremy looked at me and laughed. "That's when I knew it wasn't our great preaching that converted the village. The hurricane that destroyed the islands and brought Mike and me to Vanuatu had destroyed most of the cane the people used to build their homes. God had used us to fulfill the missionary's prophecy."

As I wrote Jeremy's story, I reflected on a portion of his favorite poem "Hound of Heaven." Francis Thompson wrote:

> I fled him, down the nights and down the days
>
> I fled him, down the arches of the years

I fled him, down the labyrinthine ways

Of my own mind and in the mist of tears

I hid from him, and under running laughter.

Up vistaed hopes I sped and shot, precipitated

Adown Titanic glooms of chasmed fears,

From those strong feet that followed followed after

But with unhurrying chase, and unperturbed pace…"

    God relentlessly pursues humanity "with unhurrying chase and unperturbed pace." Whether it takes ten years or one hundred years, God's strong feet follow until his word bears fruit in our lives.

Radically Changed

I met Bill Shanks, the pastor of New Covenant Fellowship, while filming *God Stories* at a meeting of the Greater New Orleans Pastors' Coalition. Unlike other pastors who began talking before I could position myself to record their comments, Bill paused until I had a clear shot to film him. When the meeting concluded, I asked for his card and permission to contact him.

The following week, I entered Pastor Bill's home to a disarming warmth and delightful kindness. His front door revolved with people filling his house with life. While I set up my camera, he prepared a fresh pot of coffee. I poured sugar into my coffee cup and gave him my standard spiel: "People tend to talk in random disconnected thoughts. I'll guide the conversation and interrupt to clarify. If you regret anything you say, I will not make it public." He smiled, and I pushed record.

Bill felt close to the Lord as an altar boy in the Catholic Church. By the time he married, he had drifted from his faith, but life was good. He had a decent relationship with his wife. Selling hospital equipment in a three-state area provided an adequate living for his family. He still attended Mass but only did so for the sake of his children.

On the way to a sales appointment, Bill poured out his heart to the Lord. "Why am I here? Is there a purpose for my life? Show me what you want from me."

That night, Bill checked into a hotel room. He set his suitcase on the bed and examined the sparsely furnished room. Feeling restless, he returned to his car and drove down the town's deserted streets looking for a cocktail lounge but couldn't find one. He spotted a movie theater and pulled into the parking lot. "Closed" glared the sign in the ticket window.

Bill returned to the hotel and asked the manager, "Where is everybody in this town?"

"Most of them are at the church."

"Church on a Wednesday night! Where is it?"

"Just down the street," replied the manager.

Reluctant to return to an empty hotel room, Bill went to the church. He was accustomed to the solemn reverence of a Catholic Mass. The Pentecostal church service was different. People clapped their hands to lively music. Some held both hands in the air, joy emanating from their faces. A preacher stepped behind the pulpit. He opened his Bible to the book of Revelation and read, "I know your deeds, that you are neither cold nor hot. I wish you were either one or the other! So, because you are lukewarm—neither hot nor cold—I am about to spit you out of my mouth" (Revelation 3:15-17).

The scripture sliced through Bill like a hot knife through butter challenging his belief that only murderers and thieves went to hell. The preacher's exhortation to repent at the conclusion of his message disturbed him. "I would have become a priest if I wanted to dedicate my life to God," said Bill. "I left the service without repenting, sorry that I had attended." As Bill drove back to his hotel room, a thought made him uncomfortable. *You asked God to show you what he wanted, and now you are walking away.* Bill's refusal to repent haunted him for eight months. He broke while listening to his priest talk about Jesus's sufferings. Bill returned home and searched the phone book for a Pentecostal church.

Bill laughed. "They were singing 'He Is Coming Soon' when I walked into the church. I thought they were talking about me and ran to the altar. I felt like Jesus embraced me and said, 'I've waited for you.' I left that church radically changed."

Bill questioned his priest about the experience. The priest assured Bill that he had only had an emotional experience that would fade. Bill looked at me and smiled. "That was forty years ago, and it never faded. I had never experienced love like I experienced in that church."

In the late 1980s, Bill watched *The Silent Scream*, a twenty-five-minute film documenting an abortion that created a storm of controversy and launched the international pro-life movement. The film deeply moved him. When the question was asked, "Who will speak for the unborn?" He raised his hand.

Bill worked a secular job to supplement his pastor's salary when he learned of plans to picket an abortion clinic. He decided to join the picketers on his lunch hour. "My biggest fear was someone I knew would see me," said Bill. "When some girls entering the clinic yelled at me to mind my own business, I wanted to leave. Then I heard God say, 'If you leave, babies will die.'" The thought of innocent babies dying gave Bill the strength to overcome his fear. He remained the duration of his lunch hour, pleading for the life of the unborn who could not speak for themselves.

Several months later, a friend called with an invitation. "They are putting pastors in jail for trying to save the lives of babies in Atlanta. I'm going, and I'd like you to come." Initially, Bill declined but then changed his mind and traveled to Atlanta with thirteen pastors. The pastors sat in front of the abortion clinic door, blocking the entrance. Soon, the police arrived and shouted through bullhorns, "If you don't move, you will be arrested."

"Everything in me said to move. Obey the police. Then one of the pastors said, 'If we move, they will kill babies today.'" Bill stayed. The police handcuffed the pastors and put them in the back of a paddy wagon. On the way to jail, Bill heard the Lord say, "This is the first of many times you will be arrested." Bill grew somber as he continued his story. "In that moment I realized the degenerate condition of America. Why were authorities putting us in jail for trying to save innocent babies from slaughter?"

The week Bill spent in the Atlanta jail radically changed his life. More than one-hundred inmates and guards accepted Christ as their Savior. One of the female guards asked them why they were willing to go to jail. Bill answered, "The unborn children belong to God. He has a purpose for their lives, and the children have a right to live and fulfill that purpose." The guard burst into tears. She was pregnant and planned to have an abortion.

While the authorities debated what to do with the pastors, they were sent to the hundred-year-old Hero Prison Farm. The buildings had no air conditioning or screens on the windows to keep bugs out. Roaches scurried across a makeshift altar as the pastors held a communion service with bread and water. They wept and repented for allowing the nation to slip into an immoral abyss.

As Bill awaited his fate for participating in civil disobedience fear overwhelmed him. When he marched into the courtroom with the other pastors, he remembered Jesus's words: "When you are brought before synagogues, rulers and authorities, do not worry about how you will defend yourselves or what you will say, for the Holy Spirit will teach you at that time what you should say" (Luke 12:11-12). The scripture comforted Bill and dispelled his fear.

The African American judge questioned several of the pastors and then turned his attention to Bill. "Where did you meet these men?"

"I met them in the same cell block Martin Luther King was in," said Bill.

"What's that got to do with anything?" demanded the judge.

"Sir, if he had not laid down his life for your rights, you would be cleaning this court instead of sitting in judgment."

The judge was silent for a moment and then brought his gavel down with a thud. "Case dismissed."

In the summer of 1991, Bill participated in the Summer of Mercy sponsored by Operation Rescue and Operation Save America. Dr. George Tiller had sent a letter to doctors all over the country advertising his late-term abortion services. He had developed a method called MOLD, which produced, according to Tiller, "a normal, safe, natural miscarriage." Tiller killed the baby by injecting digoxin into the baby's heart. He used Laminaria to dilate the cervix and then induced labor. Mothers of the dead babies had the option of cuddling their aborted child while a picture was taken to aid them in the grieving process. Then the bodies of the babies were thrown into an incinerator.

Bill was one of the forty thousand people who traveled to Wichita, Kansas, to protest the barbaric practice. "When Tiller turned on the incinerator, the ashes of those babies would settle all over us," said Bill, "on our bodies, on our Bibles. We planned to block the entrance while another group created a diversion by sitting in the street. The rest would go over the fence that surrounded the clinic. One of the leaders told us we would only incur a twenty-five dollar fine, but I'd been in it long enough to know this wasn't a twenty-five dollar offense."

Federal marshals arrested Bill, charged him with a felony, and incarcerated him until he could post a $10,000 bond. Pastor Larry Stockstill, Bethany Word Prayer Center, Baton Rouge, arrived a week later and bailed the Louisiana pastors out of jail.

The protest in Wichita concluded on August 25, 1991, with a rally at Cessna Stadium. Thirty-five thousand people attended the "Hope for the Heartland" rally. Pro-life activists continued to lead similar campaigns of protest and blockade in other cities until 1994. With support from Kansas senator Bob Dole, Congress passed the Federal Access to Clinics Entrances (FACE) law. The FACE law carried a federal fine of $1,000 and one year in jail for the first offense. The $10,000 fine and ten years in jail for the second offense persuaded many to abandon the campaign against abortion.

    I attended an abortion protest with Pastor Bill. He has adjusted its tactics to be more gentle and kind. From the public sidewalk, he challenged the people in the clinic to search their hearts. Then Bill and his team took turns repenting for their own sins and praying that God would grant repentance to the employees within. Women entering the clinic were offered the names of pro-life doctors and the locations of free pro-life clinics. One woman exiting the clinic hollered, "I'll kill my baby if I want to kill my baby." Her disregard for human life stood in sharp contrast to a man pleading for everyone's right to live and fulfill his or her God-given purpose.

Tarzan of Manhattan

I wanted to read *The Strange Story of Tarzan of Manhattan* before Jim Siracuse spoke at the Pot of Praise. The event organizer brought me to Jim's condominium to pick up a copy of his self-published book. Jim insisted that we stay for coffee.

The slender, well-groomed man wore his eighty-nine years well. While he prepared coffee, I read his bio on the last page of his book. He is in good health, exercises six times a week, and prays two hours daily before walking the streets of his community, sharing Jesus with anyone willing to listen. Jim wrote his book for his grandchildren. There are a limited number of copies available. I read the fascinating 250-page story of this WWII veteran in less than two days and then called Jim for permission to write an article about his spiritual journey.

When Jim fell ill as an infant, a doctor introduced Jim's father to a health fad. His father embraced the fad to the point of fanaticism. For the first twelve years of Jim's life, his diet consisted of raw fruits, vegetables, olives, and nuts. To ensure Jim received nature's natural sunshine and fresh air, his mother dutifully brought him to play in the woods at the northern tip of Manhattan. She crocheted while he ran naked in the forest from morning until sundown. A 1922 newspaper clipping about Jim titled "New York Has Tarzan Baby" is included in his book.

Jim's path to God was as unusual as his childhood. In 1944, as Jim waited to board an A-20 for a bombing mission in Amiens, France, he had a foreboding that he would not return. When his squadron approached its target, the tail of his plane took a direct hit. Then the right engine was blown away, leaving the prop spinning out of control. Jim ordered his gunners to jump. He kept his plane in formation until he dropped his bombs on the German train laden with ammunition.

Flames engulfed the plane as Jim ejected into enemy territory. He hit the ground with greater impact than he anticipated, injuring his ankle. Jim quickly gathered up his parachute to hide it from the Germans. As he hobbled toward the woods, two German soldiers on a three-wheeled motorcycle sped toward him. They sprayed machine gun bullets at Jim, but not one bullet found its target.

The soldiers brought him to their field headquarters, where an interrogator shoved his machine gun into Jim's right temple. The ammunition train he had bombed continued to explode, shaking the ground beneath their feet. A tall, blond-haired German screamed and frothed at the mouth. With each explosion, his anger intensified until Jim feared that he would pull the trigger, if not intentionally, by accident. Desperate to calm the agitated soldier, Jim did the only thing he could think of: he smiled. The soldier abruptly quit screaming and walked away.

The Germans sent Jim to Stalag Luft 3. A few months before he arrived, two hundred prisoners of war sought to escape. Through a team effort, the prisoners had simultaneously dug three tunnels named Tom, Dick, and Harry. They completed tunnel Tom, but it fell twenty feet short of the forest that was intended to provide cover. The Germans discovered their plan, and the desperate prisoners were mowed down with machine gun fire as they exited the tunnel. The few who eluded the rain of bullets were captured. Some were killed. After the war, a film was produced about the event called *The Great Escape*.

Jim's unwelcome new home in the infamous Stalag Luft 3 faced the communal latrine. "The latrine wasn't the best of neighbors, nor was the breeze what you'd call a breath of fresh air. Our room seemed to be the official headquarters, or shall we say the favorite hangout for latrine flies, swarms of them!" wrote Jim.

In this place of human suffering, Jim heard about the Bible for the first time. An army major assigned to Jim's room constantly talked about the Bible. When Jim questioned him, the major responded, "The Bible is the greatest book ever written." Jim enjoyed reading Perry Mason books and wondered if the Bible could be better.

The following year, January 1945, the Russians broke through the eastern front. Nervous soldiers screamed at the prisoners to collect their belongings. At 10:00 p.m., in seventeen-degree-below-zero weather with a foot of snow on the ground, Jim and 10,000 of his fellow POWs were forced to walk nonstop for fifty-six hours to Spremberg. They arrived barely alive and were herded like cattle onto a freight train for Mooseberg.

Jim's hope that Mooseberg would offer better living conditions proved futile. He wrote, "Mooseberg…was overrun by lice and fleas. They walked all over our bodies, twenty-four hours a day, under our clothes, in our eyes, often in our mouths, and on our food. They'd bite and cause bumps and rashes. We couldn't sleep or rest. That horrible latrine we complained about at Stalag 3 was pure luxury."

Jim borrowed a Bible from a fellow prisoner, planning to read it from cover to cover. After reading the first six pages of Genesis, he decided the major who highly recommended the Bible was crazy. Three months later, American troops liberated the POWs at Mooseberg.

Jim returned to America, where he was assigned to Craig Field in Selma, Alabama. He didn't think about the Bible again until he met Mary in the civilian cafeteria. She wasn't like the girls he usually dated. "Her personality was vivacious, humorous, with a pleasing touch of humility," wrote Jim. Mary was Baptist. Jim considered himself an agnostic, but he was curious about religion. He willingly listened as Mary shared her faith. "God works in wondrous ways," Jim told me during a phone conversation. "He arranged for this slicker from Manhattan to meet an Alabama farm girl to bring me to salvation."

Jim fell in love with Mary but decided there were too many differences between them for a marriage to work. They agreed not to pursue a serious relationship. A higher power voided their agreement on a Sunday afternoon in February of 1946. Jim and Mary were sitting on the edge of an empty swimming pool when Jim had an experience that convinced him God involves himself in the lives of his creations. Jim wrote:

> …Something suddenly gripped me! I couldn't move! The whole sky changed to a deep orange! No clouds, no variation, just a beautiful orange color as far as my eyes could see. I didn't know what was happening. I couldn't turn or talk or signal for help. I was totally immobilized, paralyzed! Then a voice said, "This is the girl you're going to marry." My heart suddenly filled with an overwhelming love for this girl sitting to my left. I never knew any emotion so strong and so pure and so compelling. The sky returned to normal. I looked at Mary. She was unaware of anything that happened."
>
> —Jim Siracuse, *The Strange Story of Tarzan of Manhattan*, 100

This time Jim read the Bible with different results. When he read John 3:16, something surged within him, and the verse seemed to leap off the page. Jim felt that God had reached out to him. Without hesitation or reluctance, he asked Jesus to come into his life. He also decided to make Mary his wife. "We married August 1946. The beginning of a fifty-three-year honeymoon," said Jim.

God is everywhere—in the depths of human suffering, in the heights of heaven, and in an ancient book that speaks to human hearts. Jim's first witness of God came in the midst of suffering created by war. His second witness came from the heavens when God gave him direction for his life. The greatest witness came to Jim through the living Word.

A Love Story

I considered approaching Max and Carla Miller, the deaf pastors at my church about writing their story, but, well, they are deaf. A friend of mine who worked as a sign language interpreter for thirty years can speak with her hands as easily as she speaks orally. I am not so gifted and was reluctant to start a conversation that I could not finish.

One Sunday I looked up from reading my church bulletin. Carla stood in front of me smiling. I smiled, wondering what to do next. Thankfully, her husband joined us. Although deaf by legal standards, Max is not profoundly deaf and is able to communicate orally and in sign language. Carla had read the article I wrote about Hosanna's children's pastor and wanted me to know how much she enjoyed it. I seized the opportunity to ask Max and Carla if they would share their testimony with me.

Max told me how he came to Christ, and then Carla told her story in sign language as Max interpreted. I had planned to write separate articles. But their story is woven so tightly together that it's hard to tell where one stopped and the other began.

Max relaxed in the student lounge at Gallaudet University (the world's only liberal arts university for the deaf), discussing religion, when his attractive, young friend, Carla Simoneaux, said, "I'm proud to be a Catholic."

"Why?" asked Max.

"Because Jesus built a church for us."

"Get out of here." Max laughed. He liked the brash young woman, but the engagement ring on her finger ruled out the possibility of anything more than friendship.

Carla wasn't the only one who talked to Max about Jesus. Ray, a friend, asked Max if he knew Jesus. "Of course I know about Jesus," replied Max.

"No," Ray said. "I'm not asking if you know about him. Do you know him personally?" Max listened quietly as Ray explained how Jesus made it possible to know God.

"I didn't take his word for it," Max said to me. "But I thought about it."

Six weeks later, a friend handed Max a Chick Tract Publication titled *Somebody Loves Me*. "The story of a child abused by his father but loved by God really touched me," said Max, "so I asked him for another tract." The next day he gave Max *Holy Joe*. The message of our inability to earn our way into heaven also touched Max, so he asked him for another one. After three weeks of reading Chick Tracts, Max entertained thoughts of becoming a Christian and attended a Bible study.

"I banged on the door," said Max. "In the deaf culture, you can't just knock. You have to turn around and use your feet to bang on the door really hard so the deaf person inside can feel the vibrations and know someone is at the door." When the door opened, Max heard the leader of the Bible study conclude his prayer with the words "and you will be saved."

The Bible study had started an hour early. The man teaching the study asked if Max would like him to share the lesson again. Max said, "Yes." The teacher opened his Bible to Acts chapter 16. Max listened intently to the story of Paul and Silas.

Paul and Silas were unjustly beaten and thrown in prison for casting a spirit of divination out of a slave girl. Instead of complaining, they prayed and sang hymns to God. Suddenly, an earthquake shook the prison, causing the cell doors to open, and the chains on the prisoner's hands and feet came loose. When the jailer saw the prison doors opened, he thought all the prisoners had escaped, so he drew his sword to kill himself.

Paul shouted for the jailer to stop and assured him no one had left the prison. The jailer brought Paul and Silas out of the prison and asked, "Sirs, what must I do to be saved?" (Acts 16:30) Paul replied, "Believe in the Lord Jesus, and you will be saved" (Acts 16:31).

The phrase "Believe in the Lord Jesus, and you will be saved" convinced Max that he should accept the salvation Jesus offered. The teacher gave him two options. He could lead Max in a prayer or Max could go in a separate room and pray for himself. Max decided to pray privately.

"I asked the Lord to forgive me, to come into my life, and to make me a new person, but I didn't feel anything. Nothing!" Max said.

When he returned from the room, Ray asked him what happened. "I gave my life to Jesus," said Max.

"Praise the Lord!" Ray shouted.

"That's it?"

"That's it," Ray assured him.

Three days later, Max was eating lunch in the school cafeteria when a friend stopped at his table and exclaimed, "What happened to you?"

"What do you mean?" asked Max.

"A few days ago your face was dark, but now your face shines like a light." Before Max could respond, his friend said, "Have a nice day," and left. Max doubted that anything had happened when he prayed for Jesus to come into his life. His friend's comment assured him that something had.

"It hit me," said Max. "We don't live on the feeling that we are saved. We know that we are."

As Max rejoiced in his newfound faith, Carla Simoneaux questioned hers. "I was faithful to the Catholic Church," said Carla, "but I wasn't a good girl. I prayed and prayed but couldn't stop sinning." Fearful she would go to hell, Carla considered becoming a nun and sent a letter requesting religious orders. As she left her teenage years, the thought of becoming a nun left also.

After her encounter with Max in the student lounge, Carla had an unusual experience in the women's dorm. One night stillness settled over her. Carla walked down the hall to see if she was alone and saw one open door.

She walked into the dorm room and talked to Mary Beth for hours before the topic of religion came up. Carla shared how frustrated she was with her efforts to please God. Mary Beth challenged Carla to return to the basic simplicity of the gospel message and encouraged her to read the Gospel of John. The following week, Carla read Matthew, Mark, Luke, and John.

Desperate to find peace with God, Carla accepted Mary Beth's invitation to attend Arlington Assembly of God. "The people were warm and friendly," said Carla. Lottie Riekehof, author of *The Joy of Signing*, led the Sunday school class Carla attended. Then Carla followed Mary Beth into the main sanctuary. At the end of the pastor's sermon, Lottie Riekehof met Carla at the altar and led her in the Sinner's Prayer. Carla smiled broadly as she said to me in sign language, "All of the worry, all of the fear, and the heavy burden of guilt rolled away. Joy filled my life. From that time to this has been wonderful."

Max and Carla reconnected during summer classes. He seized the opportunity to ask Carla for a date when he learned she had broken her engagement. Three weeks later, he asked the brash young woman who stole his heart in the student lounge at Gallaudet University to marry him.

There are times I feel nothing when I pray as Max did. I've also experienced the assurance of answered prayer as Carla did. Feelings are not trustworthy. Max and Carla's story assured me God always hears a sincere prayer.

A Burning Bush Experience

I walked into the Southern Christian Writers Guild meeting and saw an unusual sight: a man. Jim Chester, comedian, magician, and now author, learned about the meeting while performing at an event with one of the guild members. With a touch of humor, he shared his writing experience and goals. I could have listened to him talk for hours. Several months later, we met at a coffee house and I listened intently as he shared his faith.

Jim was twelve-years-old when he attended a Sunday school class that prepared him for church membership. At the end of the course, those who affirmed they understood the purpose of Jesus's life were baptized. "In retrospect, taking the class did not change my life," said Jim. "But from that time forward, if anyone asked me if I was a Christian, I would immediately say yes."

While attending college, Jim lost interest in church and explored other beliefs, primarily Daoism, due to the popularity of the 1970s television series *Kung Fu*. But God had not lost interest in Jim. His skill on the basketball court earned him an invitation to play with an intramural team organized by the Baptist Student Union. Jim spent the next three years active in the student union, where he met and later married Connie.

"Connie thought she had married a Christian," said Jim. "About a year after we married, I told her 'I love you more than anything in the world.' She said she loved me too but loved Jesus more. I blew a fuse and demanded to know how she could love Jesus more than me. That's when she began to suspect that I wasn't saved."

Marriage, college, and working full time proved difficult, so Jim dropped out of school and opened a screen printing business. The seasonal nature of the printing business compounded his frustrations. Connie, a committed Christian, encouraged Jim to seek God. Jim prayed for God to speak to him in a burning bush as Moses experienced on Mt. Sinai so he could have faith to believe in God. The heavens remained silent. Jim felt God had spurned him and relied on drugs to cope with life's disappointments.

Jim and Connie were at a party when Ray, a magician, entertained the guests. He asked Jim to choose a card from the deck, look at it, and then return it to the deck.

Ray shuffled the deck and withdrew a card. "Is this your card?" said Ray.

"No," said Jim.

Ray pulled out another card. "This is your card."

"Nope."

Ray leaned the deck against a blender full of daiquiris and walked into another room.

Jim looked at Connie. "This guy stinks." Connie gasped. Jim looked back and saw his card rising out of the deck. "This guy is great!" shouted Jim as Ray reentered the room laughing.

Jim looked at me, his face serious. "My life changed in that moment. If I had said, 'How did you do that?' he wouldn't have told me. But I said 'I'd give anything to learn how to do stuff like that.' Ray taught me magic. Within a year I was entertaining people at birthday parties."

A phone call to obtain supplies from Ray's magic shop resulted in another life-changing moment. "Ray told me his business was booming. Once again, I made a statement that changed my life: 'If you ever need any help, let me know.' At the time, Ray's business partner was looking for a store manager." Jim moved to Atlanta to manage a prestigious magic shop. A year later, Jim opened his own magic shop in the New Orleans Hyatt Regency Hotel.

His business venture proved profitable until the New Orleans Riverwalk Marketplace opened. The shops in the Hyatt began closing until Ace Magic was a lone light at the end of a dark hallway. With his business failing and his finances drained, Jim contemplated suicide.

Two things happened that turned Jim's life around. A friend gave him a construction job, and Showtime's *Funniest Man in America* contest held regional tryouts in New Orleans. "Connie suggested I enter," said Jim. "I told her I am a shopkeeper, not a comedian. She said, 'You're not much of a shopkeeper, so why not enter?'"

Jim grinned. "The *New Orleans Laugh Off* was one of fourteen regional competitions. I finished second, behind Ellen DeGeneres. Second place qualified me for the national competition, and offers to travel the comedy circuit poured in. But everyone I knew traveling the comedy circuit was divorced. I wasn't willing to sacrifice my marriage for a successful career as a comedian."

Jim continued construction work during the day and earned extra money performing magic on the weekends until he hurt his back. Several back surgeries later, working in construction ceased to be an option. Jim focused on a career as a full-time magician. He was earning enough to support his family when he sensed emptiness in his life.

Jim attended church sporadically to pacify his wife. One Sunday, he heard a sermon about intellectual Christianity. The pastor explained that some people know about Jesus but they don't have him in their hearts. Around the same time Jim heard the sermon, a friend gave him *The Christ Commission* by Og Mandino. The book examined the death and resurrection of Jesus in a similar manner to the Warren Commission's investigation of Kennedy's assassination.

The pastor's sermon had convinced Jim that he did not have Jesus in his heart. After reading *The Christ Commission*, Jim realized he had never seriously read the Bible. For the first time in his life, Jim opened a Bible, intent on learning about God.

"I read a passage in Romans that made me stop and think: '…if thou shalt confess with thy mouth the Lord Jesus, and shalt believe in thine heart that God hath raised him from the dead, thou shalt be saved' (Romans

10:9, KJV). Suddenly, I understood. Our belief justifies us, but it's by our confession that we are saved. I believed the Gospel story, but I had never confessed or even allowed Jesus to be the Lord of my life. The realization that I had to surrender my will before I could do his will was a turning point."

Jim told Connie the next time they went to church he needed to ask Jesus to come into his heart and to be his Lord. He never made it to the church altar. Connie was part of a mass choir at a Jay Strack revival being held at Slidell High School's football stadium that evening. He accompanied her to the meeting.

Jim smiled broadly. "On Tuesday night November 19, 1991, I fell under conviction when the altar call was made. I didn't know if I would still be alive next Sunday to walk the aisle in my church, so I joined the mass of teenagers at the front of the stadium. I kneeled and said, 'Lord, I'm tired. I've done everything I can do, and it's just not working. If you can do a better job, here I am. Take my life and make something out of it. I'm totally yours.' After I prayed, I felt like the weight of the world had been lifted from my shoulders."

The following year, Jim took off his wedding band while practicing baseball. When he returned home, he reached into his pocket to retrieve his ring, but it wasn't there. Jim had already lost three wedding bands and knew his wife would be furious to learn he had lost a fourth one. The following day, he returned to the baseball field to search for his ring.

Jim roamed the field, praying he would find the ring, until he grew weary. Reluctantly, he walked back to his truck. As he reached for the door handle, he noticed a light underneath his truck. He took a step back and saw his ring glowing in the middle of the truck's long, black shadow.

"The ring was glowing like a lightbulb, radiant inside and out," said Jim. "In order to reach it, I had to get on my knees. That is when I realized I was looking at my burning bush—the one I had demanded of God so many years earlier. I slipped the ring on my finger and thanked God for the miracle. Then I asked God want he wanted from me. In that moment, I knew my skill as a magician could be used in a positive way to communicate the gospel."

I pointed to Jim's wedding band. "Is that the ring that glowed?"

"Yes," said Jim, "that happened eighteen years ago, and I never lost my wedding band again."

Sometimes the answers to our prayers are delayed because our relationship with God is out of sync. Jim demanded a sign that he thought proved God's love. But Moses's experience at the burning bush was a call to service. God could not give Jim what he demanded until Jim recognized Jesus as a Lord to be obeyed. When Jim yielded his life to God, he found his burning bush in a symbol of mutual love and commitment.

Is That All There Is?

We were reading excerpts from our work at the Southern Christian Writers Guild. One resourceful writer enlisted Sandy Cash to sing the musician's part in her story. I thought an angel fell from heaven's choir. I asked Sandy if she would share her spiritual journey with me. The vivacious blonde with snappy blue eyes often broke into song as she told a story of tragedy and triumph.

Sandy had loved music as long as she could remember and dreamed of being a star. After she graduated from high school, she dated a race car driver. "The kind with the parachute on the back to stop the car," she said. She often sang with the radio when they went on dates. One day he asked Sandy if she would like to audition for his brother's blues band.

Sandy grew up singing country but improvised a blues song. The band hired her on the spot. She traveled with them, singing a mix of Janis Joplin and Carol King songs until work ran out. Sandy returned home and found work with The Good Life, which resulted in a national recording contact with Scepter Records. For the next three-and-a-half years, she sang in five-star hotels. "We traveled to all kinds of wonderful places," said Sandy, "a real nice career for a young woman starting out in show business."

When the band broke up, Sandy returned to Florida to live with her mother. While lying on the beach, Sandy saw a cruise ship sail by and wondered if there were rock bands on the ships. She called the cruise line, and the company hired her as a band leader. Sandy's impromptu call in search of a job set her on a path to a dramatic encounter with God.

Linda, an employee on the ship's entertainment staff, shared her faith with Sandy. Sandy was happy with her career choice and wasn't interested in following Jesus. "My grandmother told me the entertainment industry was evil. She would turn over in her grave if she knew a jazz dancer told me about Jesus." Sandy laughed.

Linda's persistence met a brick wall of resistance. As a last resort, she gave Sandy *The Way*, a Bible written in everyday language that read like a novel. Sandy relented and began reading the Bible. About the same time, a Christian group chartered the ship. Sandy made a habit of talking to passengers, hoping to receive positive comments on the evaluation sheets they filled out at the end of the cruise. She was attracted to some men who were in a gospel singing group and made it a point to talk to them during her breaks. "Not because they were gospel," said Sandy. "They liked me and they were singers."

One night Sandy saw Pedro, her boyfriend, who also worked on the ship, glaring at her as she talked to the singers. She didn't understand his anger. Talking to passengers was part of her job. At the end of the cruise, Sandy was on the way to her cabin when a waitress told her Pedro fought with one of the singers. When Pedro came to her cabin, she rebuked him for his jealousy. He became enraged and raised his fist. Sandy cried out in her heart *God, what do I do?* A still, small voice said, *Act like you are not afraid.* Pedro's fist whizzed by Sandy's head and slammed into the wall. Sandy dared not move as Pedro repeatedly slammed his fist and head into the wall until he was exhausted.

The next morning, Pedro announced they needed a break from one another, but Sandy knew she needed more than a break. She feared Pedro would slam his fist into her face the next time his anger flared. She also knew severing her relationship with Pedro would be impossible as long as they worked on the same ship.

Sandy discussed her predicament with her band. They agreed to buy her equipment and finish her contract with the cruise line. When she was free to leave the ship, reality set in—no job, no place to go, no equipment to start over. Distressed, Sandy walked onto the promenade deck of the ship and confessed to God that her sins had brought this disaster upon her.

Sandy's chin quivered, and tears streamed down her face as she explained to me what happened next. "A rainbow dropped onto the bow of the ship, and a supernatural feeling swept over me. Then I heard God say, 'I forgive you. I love you. Everything will be all right.' It was the most incredible thing that had ever happened to me."

Sandy's mother picked her up at the terminal. On their way home, Sandy told her mother what had happened on the deck of the cruise ship. Her mother exclaimed, "Sandy, you've been born again." Sandy asked her mother what God expected her to do. "You stop sinning and go to church," her mother affirmed.

Sandy attended church and sought God for direction for her life. The guidance she needed came when Sandy met a friend for coffee to discuss if she should return to her entertainment career. Her friend said, "Sandy, it doesn't matter what you do. God will never leave you or forsake you."

Longing to sing again, Sandy contacted the cruise lines to see if she could return. The company assigned her to a different ship as a principal entertainer and tripled her salary. Sandy was thrilled, except for the nagging guilt that returning to her career had offended God.

The first night on the ship, Sandy's smile hid the torment raging within her as she introduced passengers at the captain's cocktail party. Thoughts that she had willingly returned to a den of iniquity and was now headed for hell whipped her mercilessly until she panicked. Sandy looked down the line of passengers and spotted a woman she had seen at embarkation wearing a large cross. She walked quickly to the woman and asked, "Do you know Jesus?"

The guest looked at the distraught woman standing in front of her and smiled. "I sure do, honey." Mary put her arm around Sandy's shoulder and steered her to the woman's restroom. She listened quietly as Sandy shared her born-again experience and her fear that she had sinned when she returned to her career.

"Meeting Mary was a divine appointment," said Sandy. "She comforted me and assured me of God's love."

For the next five years, Sandy traveled to Hollywood in between tours on the cruise ship, seeking to become a star. "If I hadn't been born again," said Sandy, "Hollywood would have devoured me." Sandy's dream eluded her until the Hilton Hotel in New Orleans hired her Jazz trio. "The gig at the Hilton lasted for eight years," said Sandy. "A gig lasting that long is unheard of in show business."

During her gig at the Hilton, her desire to open shows for famous entertainers found its fulfillment. Sandy opened for The Commodores, Al Hirt, Pete Fountain, and then Bob Hope's agent called Sandy's agent. He needed a singer with a girl-next-door image to open for Bob Hope. Sandy had already prepared to be an opening act for a superstar by paying arrangers to write big band charts for her alto voice. "If I had not already purchased the arrangements, I wouldn't have been able to fulfill the gig with Bob Hope," said Sandy.

When the big night arrived, Sandy was escorted to her dressing room and saw a star on the door. Her personal pianist and bass player accompanied her onto the stage, where a forty-piece orchestra awaited her arrival. She smoothed her $500 gown, surveyed the audience of four thousand, and then began her fifteen-minute warm-up for Bob Hope. She sang for thirty minutes. Bob Hope was late. Sandy walked off the stage feeling God had showered his love upon her.

Overwhelmed with gratitude that God had made her a star, she returned to the empty auditorium clad in jeans and sneakers to savor her fame. Instead of recapturing the moment, she stood on a dark stage and felt loneliness. Sandy prayed. "God, is that all there is?"

The sweet voice of the Holy Spirit whispered, "That's all there is. Will you let me be the superstar in your life, Sandy?"

This time Sandy abandoned her entertainment career to seek the fulfillment in following Jesus and traveled as an evangelist for many years. God's work in her life contrasted religion with the steady hand of God's love. Religion is consumed with touch not, taste not, handle not, and the ever present threat of hell for the disobedient. Love patiently waits for us to discover the vanity of human ambition and then steps in to be our superstar.

The Lost Boys

A friend and fellow blogger introduced me to The Rivers of Kush Trading Company, a missionary venture striving to improve the life of people living in the Nuba Mountains of Sudan. When I expressed a desire to write about the Trading Company, she referred me to Jack Slater Armstrong, the company's director of international communications, who graciously agreed to meet me for lunch.

"My father was an Episcopal priest," said Slater. "I understood the need to receive Jesus as Savior and Lord. But I didn't recognize his Lordship over my life until I was fifteen. That's when God filled me with his Spirit at a Faith Alive weekend."

Slater's commitment to Christ coincided with the rise of contemporary Christian music as a profitable industry. He set a goal to become a famous Christian recording artist, but God gently redirected Slater's ambition. While driving to an all-day music concert in Dallas, Texas, Slater heard Steve Fry sing "We Can Change the World."

"That song really struck a chord in my heart," said Slater. The following month, he traveled to Estes Park, Colorado, to attend the National Music Seminar for Christian Artists. During the seminar, Larry Norman, the father of Christian rock; Steve Fry; and other famous musicians addressed the detrimental direction the Christian music industry had taken. Their message opened Slater's eyes to the shallowness of pursuing fame, and he prayed for direction.

"I'm a night person and don't usually go to morning things," Slater continued, "but the last day of the seminar, a friend asked me to attend a morning session conducted by Youth With A Mission." During the session, the founder of the music company at the Montana YWAM base amazed Slater with stories of God's power. "I wanted to talk to her after the session," said Slater, "but the line was long and I wasn't sure it was for me. I left several times but came back. After I returned for the third time, Mrs. Foye announced that she had to leave. Before she walked out of the room, she prayed for us, and I heard the Lord say, 'This is what I want you to do.'"

Slater moved to Montana and spent eight years ministering as a music evangelist. During the summer, he traveled with teams of musicians to perform all over the world, including Japan, Singapore, Hong Kong, Taiwan, Australia, Belgium, Ireland, France, Scotland, and Canada. He also began a touring ministry in the United States called Troubadour to challenge the Episcopal Church to play a role in reaching impoverished people with the gospel.

In 1997, Slater attended the New Wineskins for Global Mission Conference. Marc Nikkel, a missionary priest to Sudan, Bishop Nathaniel Garang of Bor Diocese, and the Reverend Bartholomeyo Bol Deng shared the miraculous story of the Lost Boys of Sudan and the horrors of genocide. "Their message and the child-sized, coffin-shaped box containing hand-carved crosses decorated with shrapnel and empty cartridges by the Dinka Christians broke my heart," said Slater. "God and I had a conversation that went something like this:

'Why don't you do something about this?'

'Why don't you do something about it?' the Lord replied.

'I don't have money, power, or influence, not even a job. What can I do?'

'What have I given you?'

'Music and a heart that worships you.'

'I want you to make the worship of the Christians in Sudan accessible to the church in the West. They need to hear it!'"

Slater's encounter with God at the mission conference set him on a path to work in advocacy for Christians in Sudan. In 1999, he made his first trip to South Sudan to record the Sudanese Christians worshiping the Lord. Their songs are featured on *Even in Sorrow*, which Slater produced and financed. In 2003 and 2006, he traveled to the Nuba Mountains to record Christians among the tribes who descended from the ancient Nile River civilizations of Kush.

We often stray as we pursue God. Blinded by ambition, we reach for gold and discover, sometimes too late, that we only have pyrite. Slater obeyed the Holy Spirit's direction for his life and escaped the disappointment of fool's gold without losing his heart's desire. As Slater pursued a higher calling, God fulfilled his desire to be a national recording artist. He was featured on *Integrity's Intimate Worship* album (2000). The songs

Slater recorded for that album were later rereleased on seventeen compilation CDs, including *Hymns4Worship* (2004) and *Heaven* (2007).

Treasure in Cell #7

A pastor gave me information to put on NOLA's faith blog about an outreach program that his church was sponsoring. I wasn't able to post the information before the event, so I attended the outreach to take photos and to write an article. When I arrived, gray-haired men wearing black shirts announcing Jesus Outreach Ministries were showing a handful of curious young men scriptures in the Bible.

The setup was fairly impressive. A lunch truck served free food while a band belted worship songs from a flatbed truck. Even the seating was covered to shelter the audience from the sun. I sat under the shelter across from the guest evangelist, Donald Eskine, who told me an intriguing story. The humility and lack of bitterness in the ex-convict sitting in front of me was impressive.

Donald's parents divorced when he was three years old. Unable to care for Donald and his siblings, his mother left them in the custody of Catholic Charities. Three years later, she returned to claim her children. Desperate to reunite her family, she had accepted a job as a barmaid, and the state returned her children to her custody.

Donald's mother had never tasted beer before she began pouring them for patrons. She died an alcoholic in denial. "I remember sitting on the steps of our house that my mother was too drunk to walk up and watching her relieve herself in the garbage can. I was ashamed," said Donald.

Donald's greatest hurt came not from his mother but the father who abandoned him. He didn't understand why his friend's father came to visit him. Donald's father never came to spend time with him. One day he tagged along like a stray dog so he could see what it was like to have a father. The man graciously allowed Donald to join them, but he also made it clear that the next time only his sons were welcome.

The rejection deeply wounded Donald, so he sought out the company of older boys in his neighborhood. Yearning for acceptance, he quit school and joined his new friends in illegal activities. The authorities picked him up for truancy and sent him to juvenile court.

The judge stared down at Donald. "Will you go to school?"

Before Donald could answer, his mother shouted, "Don't give him another chance. Lock him up. That's one less mouth I'll have to feed."

The judge sent Donald to a reform school, where he received an education in drug use from the other residents. He learned how to shoot up heroin by the time he was fifteen. His friends called him Spike, because he was so good at hitting their veins with the needle.

Donald went from one juvenile institution to another until he became an adult, and then he made the rounds in the local parish prisons. In 1980, he was sentenced to three years in federal prison for mail fraud and credit card theft. The day he was released, he returned to heroin in a quest to numb the emotional pain in his life.

Three years later, Donald returned to jail for simple burglary. "When the door slammed shut on cell number seventeen, I rolled up in a blanket and slid under the bunk," said Donald. "For four days, I laid in my own filth as my body went through withdrawal, and then I showered and cleaned my cell. The following week, a guard came to our area and announced, 'Church service.' I decided to see what happened in church and stood against the wall with nine men."

Donald followed the guard to a small room with a broken desk and some metal chairs. He listened to Johnny, an eighty-year-old former Gideon, tell a familiar story that began during Prohibition. Johnny became a sailor when he was seventeen. Whenever his ship returned to port, he bought two bottles of illegal whiskey, picked up a woman, and partied all night. One night Johnny awoke from a drunken stupor to an empty hotel room. He sat on the edge of the bed and contemplated suicide. Out of the corner of his eye, he saw a Bible on the nightstand and picked it up. Once Johnny started reading, he lost track of time. When he looked up, the sun was shining through a split in the curtain. As the light washed over his face, he suddenly understood that God offers sinful people a new life.

"Johnny's story sounded like mine," said Donald. "The only difference was booze instead of dope. I went back to my cell determined to find Johnny's God."

Donald began reading the Bible, but shortly after his decision to find God, he was released from prison. When the guard called his name and told him to pack his things, Donald tossed the Bible on his bunk and hurried out the door. Three days later, he stuck a heroin-filled needle in his arm. "I was like a dog returning to his vomit," said Donald. It wasn't long before Donald found himself in prison cell number seven rolled up in a blanket under his bunk. As his body shook with convulsions, he listened to the other prisoners mock him. "There is no God," they shouted. "The Bible is nothing but fairy tales."

Donald slid out from under his bunk to shower. When he returned, he saw a Bible lying on his bunk and became enraged with God. "Why have you made me like this?" Donald seethed, and then he broke and began sobbing. "I didn't care who heard me. I wanted to find God and prayed 'God, if you are really a living God and this is your Word, reveal it to me. If not, leave me alone and let me die the way I am.'" Excitement built in Donald's voice as he continued his story. "God heard my cry. I heard him say, 'Donald, turn to the book of Proverbs.'"

Donald used the index to find Proverbs chapter 1, where he began reading. When he reached chapter 2 and read "My Son," the words exploded within him. "God chose the most devastating hurt of my life to reveal himself to me," said Donald, "and then he told me how to find him in the first five verses of chapter 2."

> My son, if you accept my words and store up my commands within you, turning your ear to wisdom and applying your heart to understanding, and if you call out for insight and cry aloud for understanding, and if you look for it as for silver and search for it as for hidden treasure, then you will understand the fear of the Lord and find the knowledge of God.
>
> Proverbs 2:1-5

Donald looked me in the eye, his face beaming. "Most treasure hunters look for treasure their whole life and never find it. I found my treasure in cell number seven on May 13, 1987, at 9:36 p.m."

Some people find their way to a better life and others don't. Donald wasn't the only one who had heard about God. His fellow prisoners mocked God's existence. Jesus said, "Ask and it will be given to you; seek and you will find." Donald asked, and God answered. He sought God, and he found him. Those who mock God never will.

From Montreal to Ottawa

We had just ordered a feast of ribs, steaks, and potatoes at the Texas Roadhouse when a man handed us a placard suggesting donations for various balloon creatures. He instantly had my husband's attention, but not mine. Busy cracking peanuts for my granddaughter, I paid little attention to the snippets of magic tricks and science experiments with spiritual applications that intruded into my consciousness.

"What are we doing Saturday?" My husband asked me—his personal secretary and wife. I looked at him. The silent question mark was understood. "Ken is a missionary. He wants me to show him some of my science experiments."

The grinning Kenneth Landriault—clown, magician, balloon artist, and missionary to the poor—now had my full attention. "We'd love to have you come to our home, but only if you tell me how you became a missionary."

Ken loved being an altar boy in the Catholic Church but never read the Bible. During his teenage years, he abandoned the church to immerse himself in spiritual philosophies. He was well versed in the eastern "-isms" and practiced meditation when he enrolled in Quebec's exclusive Bishop's College to study dentistry.

He quickly lost interest in dentistry, pursued law, and then abandoned law to become an accountant.

"My father and his brothers were administrators and accountants," said Ken, "so I concluded it was my destiny to follow in their footsteps. I took Spanish as an elective my last year in university. Ironically, I used Spanish more than any other course I took."

Six months before Ken attended a seminar with the popular guru Bhagwan Shree Rajneesh, also known as OSHO, he was meditating in the forest behind the university. Suddenly, an image of Ken as a Catholic missionary priest replaced the visual beauty of the forest.

"It was little more than a flash in my mind. I rejected the thought, but it was very strong and clearly from God. I think I saw myself as a Catholic priest because that was all I knew at the time, so that was the way my mind interpreted the vision."

Ken traveled to America to attend the ten-day Hindu seminar and studied extreme meditation. The physically demanding form of meditation had Ken jumping up and down to the point of exhaustion or Sufi whirling until he fell into a trance. Every time Ken entered a trance, he had an experience with Jesus. During a course on astral travel, Ken lay on the floor listening to the guru speak calming words in a quest to guide his students out of their bodies.

"When I reached the point I felt my spirit leaving my body, a vivid image of Jesus appeared, breaking my concentration. Jesus didn't say anything. He didn't have to. The disapproval on his face told me I was doing something wrong."

The guru explained to Ken that Jesus was not real. To stop the interruptions, Ken needed to overcome his Catholic background that produced familiar images in his mind. As Ken returned to his place on the floor, he remembered a scripture from the Bible he had heard while attending the Catholic Church: "I am the door of the sheep. All that ever came before me are thieves and robbers: but the sheep did not hear them" (John 10:7-8, KJV). The disapproving face of Jesus was so strong Ken wondered if he was going the wrong way in his quest for spiritual enlightenment.

On the seventh day of the seminar, Bhagwan Shree Rajneesh arrived to an amazing display of affection. Ken watched in amazement as the attendees bowed before the guru. Ken could not bring himself to join them. He felt it was wrong to worship people. That night, Rajneesh sat on a throne wearing a beautiful gown and taught them that he was the modern-day door to eternity.

"I wondered how both Rajneesh and Jesus could be the door. All of a sudden, other verses warning us to beware of people who love flowing robes, sitting in places of honor, and to be called teacher came to my mind. Here I was, in a room with three hundred people hanging on every word this man said as he claimed to be the Savior of the world. At that point, I decided Jesus must be the door because he warned of things that were happening right now. I had never studied the Bible, but I had heard scriptures spoken in church. It is amazing how God's Word will stay with you" (Matthew 23:7-8, Luke 20:46).

Ken canceled his plans to travel to India with Rajneesh, returned to Montreal, and made plans to travel the world until he found the truth. That night Ken dreamed he was playing chess in a palace made of smooth clear glass. One of the chess pieces fell to the ground. He rose to retrieve the piece. As Ken moved toward the chess piece, the piece moved away, and Ken realized he would never reach it.

"That is when I heard the voice of Rajneesh call to me out of a flame of fire. I didn't want to go into the fire with Rajneesh but could not stop moving toward the flame. Suddenly, I cried out 'Jesus' as loud as I could, and I woke. Not long after that experience, God dramatically changed my life," said Ken.

Ken started reading the book *What Jesus Had to Say*. He threw the book away, mumbling, "I can't live this." Later that evening, he retrieved it from the garbage and read it for a few more days, then threw it away again. The third time he rescued the book from the garbage he read, "Jesus looked at him and loved him. 'One thing you lack,' he said. 'Go, sell everything you have and give to the poor, and you will have treasure in heaven. Then come, follow me'" (Mark 10:21). Ken liquidated his bank account, paid all his debts, and took the remaining funds to a charity in Ottawa.

"I walked into a little office furnished with one small desk, clutching the last of my earthly possessions. The secretary took the money, threw it in a drawer, and continued writing without speaking a word. She didn't even say thank you, just left me standing there. I remember thinking my money would never get to the poor, but the deed was done."

Ken walked out of the tiny office and went to the University of Ottawa to set up a back-up plan. If his trip around the world to find the truth failed, he would finish his last year of college with a scholarship the university had awarded him. He enrolled in the fall semester, chose a dorm room, and toured the campus. He walked out of the science building and into a Christian group, passing out gospel tracts. He liked arguing philosophies, but the woman who gave him a tract was pretty. He didn't want to ruin her day, so he listened politely as she said, "I have a Bible verse for you." She opened her Bible to Ephesians chapter 2 and pointed to a verse. "For it is by grace you have been saved, through faith—and this not from yourselves, it is the gift of God—not by works, so that no one can boast" (Ephesians 2:8-9).

"I think if she had showed me any other verse it would not have affected me. I no longer followed Rajneesh, but I still adhered to Hindu teachings and believed that I could purify myself through works to merge with God. The verse in Ephesians taught the opposite of everything I believed. Instead of working my way to God, he offered himself as a gift. That verse was so deep, so beautiful, so radical it hit me like a truck."

"I am getting another verse for you," said the woman. She flipped the pages of her Bible to Revelation. "Behold I stand at the door and knock if any man hear my voice and open the door I will come in to him and sup with him and he with me" (Revelation 3:20, KJV).

"Wait a minute," Ken said. "I'm only talking to you because you are beautiful. I don't believe this stuff."

"I saw you come out of the science building. Therefore, you must believe in science."

"Yes, I do."

"If you believe in science, then you believe in experimentation."

"I surely do."

"Let's do an experiment. You pray with me. If it's not true and there is no change in your life, then you have not lost anything. If Jesus comes into your heart and there is a change in your life, then you will know the Bible is true."

"Okay, as an experiment, I agree. Let's do it."

Ken looked at me and laughed. "She was very clever. I closed my eyes and asked Jesus to come into my heart. In that moment, God transformed me. When I opened my eyes, everything was different. Everything looked brighter, and I felt love for everyone. She saw the change in my countenance and invited me to a Bible study at her house."

Ken sat in the back of the Bible study, listening intently as she read from John chapter 3:

"He came to Jesus at night and said, 'Rabbi, we know you are a teacher who has come from God. For no one could perform the miraculous signs you are doing if God were not with him.' In reply Jesus declared, 'I tell you the truth, no one can see the kingdom of God unless he is born again'" (John 3:2-3).

Ken leaped to his feet. "It doesn't say that."

"Oh yes, it does."

"It can't," said Ken.

"Come and see."

Ken walked to the front of the Bible study and looked in her Bible. "This is exactly word-for-word what I experienced today. I felt like a baby. Like a child at peace and free of any worries. This is exactly what happened to me."

Ken looked at me and smiled. My trip around the world to discover the truth was short. It only took me from Montreal to Ottawa.

The Creative Dramatist

The subject line said "Christian Comedy." I didn't know the sender, but she had my interest. I opened the e-mail and read: "Teena, Please check out my new website for Women's Christian Comedy. Thanks, Kathy Frady."

Seven Kathy Fradys stared at me from the banner of her website. With little more than a wig and accessories, Kathy had created a cornucopia of characters with distinct personalities. I contacted Kathy. Two weeks later, the real Kathy Frady met me at a café.

At the tender age of nine, a concerned Christian asked Kathy if she wanted to go to hell. She immediately replied *no*. Kathy was marched into the presence of the pastor's wife. She looked up at the formidable woman, who looked down at her and said, "Do you want to go to hell?" Terrified, Kathy reaffirmed that she did not want to "go to hell." The pastor's wife led Kathy in a prayer, and the following Sunday the pastor baptized Kathy. She emerged from the baptismal tank thinking she had met God's demands to receive salvation.

Kathy knew the terror of God but remained unaware of his great love for her. Four years later, she heard friends in her youth group talk about a God who gave them peace. They rarely spoke about hell but had much to say about a personal relationship with God. Deeply convicted by the love radiating from her friends, Kathy became painfully aware of the deficiency in her own relationship with God.

For several years, God tugged at Kathy's heart to make a sincere commitment to him. She came to a breaking point at a church camp. Kathy sat on the top bunk wrestling with God when her camp counselor asked, "Is there something wrong?" Her first inclination was to lie. Weary of her struggle, Kathy blurted out the truth. "I need to know how to be a Christian."

God had already prepared the counselor to meet Kathy's need. The previous day, the counselor had discussed with a friend how to lead the children at camp to salvation and highlighted the scriptures she needed. The counselor showed her Romans 3:23 to prove that everyone has broken God's laws, then turned the pages to Romans 6:23 and showed her the result of sin is separation from God. Kathy understood from John 3:16 that Christ died for the whole world and then saw in Romans 10:9-10 that she could have a restored relationship with God. Kathy believed the scriptures she read with her counselor and made a decision to accept a loving Christ.

Kathy discovered drama while in high school. Her first experience on stage playing the part of a drama teacher foretold her future. As she memorized lines and learned how to walk across the stage, to use gestures, and to project her voice, she fell in love with acting. She founded "The Creative Dramatist" in 2006 to communicate gospel insights in a nonthreatening, fun way. When I met with Kathy, eighteen different characters were available for ministry, with new ones developed as needed. She created Rozlyn Cartwright, a self-obsessed news reporter who rambles about mint chocolate in the middle of interviews for NOLA's Faith Blog. I titled the videos "On the Road with Rozlyn." Kathy, aka Rozlyn, never failed to catch her victims off guard for some hilarious interviews.

One day, Kathy called to ask me if I could film her interviewing herself.

"What do you mean?" I asked.

Kathy explained. "I'm on a committee promoting a Beth Moore event coming to New Orleans."

"Do you think Beth Moore would consent to an interview with Rozlyn Cartwright for the faith blog?"

"Not a chance, Teena. The Chairman of the committee made it very clear that none of us would meet Beth Moore. I was thinking Rozlyn could interview my new character, Beth Mooreso."

Kathy arrived early the next morning with the accessories for Beth Mooreso. Whatever Beth Moore thought she was, Kathy's new character was that and more. We spent the day filming, first Rozlyn's lines and then Beth Mooreso's lines. We edited. Didn't like it. Filmed again. Edited again. By the time Kathy's husband arrived to pick her up, she was exhausted, but we were proud of our Beth Moore spoof.

The following month, I filmed Rozlyn's interview with Lifeway's event coordinator about the Beth Moore Living Proof Live event. Kathy gave a copy of the promotional spoof to the event coordinator. I wasn't able to attend the event and called Kathy later that week.

"I met Beth Moore," exclaimed Kathy.

"I thought they told you no one would meet Beth Moore."

"I know, but she wanted to see the spoof we made."

"On the Road with Rozlyn" had a short life span. I didn't have the equipment to produce the videos that Kathy's talent deserved. The Spirit's tug to focus on writing led me to abandon the project after we made fifteen videos.

Kathy's simple faith and sincere devotion to Christ enriched my life. I've often reflected on her salvation experience. We can't deny the existence of hell. The Bible is clear about a place of eternal damnation. We can question the tactic of using hell to force people into heaven. When well-intentioned Christians pointed to the terror of hell, she only went through the motions of salvation that left her distant and disconnected. God's loving-kindness led her to true repentance.

She's Not in Kansas Anymore

Myrinda Warner grew up on the plains of Kansas at an Angus cattle ranch. She loved staying up all night baling hay with her father. Myrinda drove a little Massey-Ferguson Tractor, and her father a John Deere. Her father's stash of Mountain Dew kept them awake when their eyes grew heavy with sleep.

Life on the ranch kept her busy, making her church attendance sporadic. "I always felt like I was looking for something," said Myrinda. "I didn't know what and went through a season of questioning God's existence." Myrinda's mother prayed for her daughter, but for many years it appeared as if God had turned a deaf ear.

During her first two years at a community college, Myrinda battled an overwhelming anxiety. She consulted a psychologist and had a physical examination. Nothing the doctors recommended helped. By her third year at college, her anxiety was so severe that she could not eat, often felt sick, and at times thought she would have to leave in the middle of class. Desperate for help, Myrinda accepted an invitation to attend a Chi Alpha Christian Fellowship meeting. She concluded that the people at the fellowship only wanted to convert her and didn't return.

Myrinda returned home for Christmas vacation but could not forget the things she learned at the Chi

Alpha meeting. When she found one of her mother's gospel tracts lying on a table, she decided to pray the Sinner's Prayer printed on the last page. "I asked God to do something in my life if he really existed," said Myrinda, "and then made a commitment to read the Bible and see if anything would happen."

When Myrinda returned for the spring semester, she moved in with the friend who had invited her to the Chi Alpha meeting. Myrinda did not plan to participate in the larger Chi Alpha meetings but was comfortable attending the smaller Bible study that her roommate had started in their dorm room. "I found the people who attended the Bible study to be the most genuine people I had ever met," said Myrinda. "When they prayed, they believed Jesus was alive and listening."

Myrinda realized how much she had changed when she attended a prayer meeting alone. Normally, her anxiety would have prevented her from going. "I asked them to pray for me but didn't tell them why. The elderly man who prayed for me said, 'God, help her not to be anxious about social interactions.'" His prayer comforted Myrinda and gave her the assurance God knew about her struggle.

One day Myrinda realized she no longer feared social gatherings. The nausea she felt during class disappeared. Making new friends came easily. She had planned to teach when she graduated but now longed to be a missionary.

The year after she graduated, Hurricane Katrina devastated the Gulf Coast. As Myrinda watched the national news coverage, she felt an urgency to help the people of New Orleans. She contacted the Red Cross to volunteer. The organization would not accept her until she completed its disaster training class. While Myrinda waited for another class to be offered, Hurricane Rita caused more devastation in Louisiana. Her urgency to help intensified, but the Red Cross still didn't have a class available. Then a guest speaker came to Myrinda's church with news of an interdenominational effort to send relief teams to the Gulf Coast. Myrinda volunteered.

October 2005, she arrived in New Orleans with seven team members. When she wasn't busy gutting houses, she was handing out water and hygiene products. "I had worked hard on my father's ranch, but it was nothing compared to cleaning out houses damaged by Katrina," said Myrinda. She wanted to stay in New Orleans, but commitments in Kansas forced her to leave.

She returned to New Orleans again in December 2005 and in March 2006. Each time Myrinda came to New Orleans, it was more difficult for her to leave. By the time she returned to New Orleans in August 2006 for a four-month commitment as a relief worker, she was making plans to stay.

God fulfilled her desire to be a missionary when Pastor Anthony invited the relief workers to his home for a hot meal and Bible study. She accepted his invitation and quickly bonded with the Christians who attended the weekly study. Her future was uncertain when she returned home for Christmas. God opened a door for her to remain in New Orleans when Pastor

Anthony's assistant telephoned and invited her to become part of a church planting team. The pastors and staff pioneering the church were full-time missionaries. She leaped at the opportunity to join them.

Myrinda began her missionary work helping the homeless in the tent city that housed the victims of Katrina's wrath. The city eventually found shelter for the tent dwellers. When the last tent was taken down, she walked the streets of New Orleans, sharing Jesus with anyone who would listen.

"God continues to amaze me by his obvious hand on my life," said Myrinda. "He gave me a passion to love the unloved, to seek out the lost, and restore hope to the hopeless."

When Myrinda's anxiety grew unbearable, she sought the wisdom of man. Their advice failed to help. In desperation, she turned to God for a solution and found the help she needed.

God's Family

Jeff and Jennifer Oettle's family had grown both in size and number since the last time I saw them. Their three daughters had sprouted like towering sunflowers. Perched on Jennifer's hip was a beautiful Haitian toddler named Judah, who bore a striking resemblance to the late actor Gary Coleman. My husband collected an assortment of toys from his study to entertain the children while the Oettles shared their adoption adventure with me.

Jeff was pursuing his dream of being a navy pilot when he attended Riverdale Church of God. During the service, Jeff witnessed a tumor the size of a grapefruit disappear from the side of an elderly woman's face. "She didn't even flinch," said Jeff. "I don't know if she even noticed the tumor was gone. When I saw it disappear, I became keenly aware God is real, God was present, and I was not right with God." As Jeff wept tears of repentance, he knew that he would leave the navy and enter the ministry.

The navy stationed Jeff in Florida shortly before the Pensacola outpouring started at Brownsville Assembly of God on Father's Day, 1995. Jennifer's parents had been members of Brownsville Assembly of God from its founding and were present the day the five-year revival started. She called her parents from work that Sunday afternoon and was shocked to learn they were still at church. Jennifer had strayed from her faith but desired a relationship with God. "I could not deny the presence of God when I attended the revival. But I wasn't ready to yield my life to God and never went to the altar," said Jennifer. "My life changed after I met Jeff."

Jeff had seen Jennifer at the services and prayed nine months before he spoke to her for the first time. "Jeff said things only God knew about me. I felt like God was speaking to me through him. Then Jeff asked me to make a commitment to attend every service for two weeks. That was a big commitment. During the revival, the church held four services a week. I kept my commitment, and God changed me. Five months later, Jeff asked me to marry him."

Before they married, Jennifer told Jeff how the desire to adopt had been planted in her heart when she was eight years old. Her best friend had been abused before she was placed in foster care and then made eligible for adoption. Jennifer saw the difference being adopted into a loving home had made in her friend's life and wanted to help a child, just as her friend had been helped.

Tragedy struck when the Oettles' first child was stillborn. The grief of losing their firstborn was soon replaced by the birth of three daughters. Jennifer suffered complications during the subsequent pregnancies, increasing her risk for heart attack or stroke. After the birth of their third child, the doctor recommended that Jennifer have her tubes tied. The Oettles agreed to the procedure.

"Unable to bear any more children, the only option to increase our family was adoption," said Jennifer.

"Even though we had three girls, I didn't have a preference about sex, age, or race. I searched for years but didn't pursue adoption because we didn't have the money. I was ready to give up when I received a phone call that changed my mind."

Melissa, a friend of Jennifer's, was in the process of adopting two children from a Christian orphanage in Haiti when the need for $5,000 stalled the process. While Melissa and her husband were visiting the church that they grew up in, a woman gave them a check for $5,000. Melissa was so excited she called Jennifer.

"God had supplied Melissa's need, and that gave me faith God would supply what I needed," said Jennifer. "I didn't know it at the time, but I received that phone call the same month Judah was born."

Jennifer had been in contact with an agency in Texas about adoption. They regularly sent her photos of available children. She kept the photos in a folder, waiting for God to quicken her heart to the child he wanted her to adopt. One day she opened an e-mail from the agency with the photo of three siblings from India.

"When I saw those children, I felt pregnant. They consumed my thoughts, but I was reluctant to tell Jeff I wanted to double our family. My girls saw me looking at the picture of the Indian children and said we needed to adopt them. That gave me the strength to present it to Jeff."

"I wondered how I would feed six children, but we decided to take a step of faith and trust God to guide us," said Jeff.

The Oettles had two weeks to raise the necessary funds to start the adoption process. The money they collected fell short of the $2,500 they needed to put a hold on the children. Then another couple applied to adopt them. While the Oettles grieved over the lost opportunity, Jennifer received a photo from Grace Children Adoption Home in Port-de-Paix, Haiti, of eight-month-old Judah.

Jeff, now a senior pastor, had already scheduled Keith and Cindy Lashbrook, the missionaries who founded the adoption home in Haiti, as guest speakers. One of the women in the congregation was deeply moved by the Lashbrooks' presentation. She requested permission to assemble a team for a mission trip to Haiti. Jeff and Jennifer traveled to Port-de-Paix the first week of December 2008 to make arrangements for the trip. "That's when Jeff and I met Judah. We belonged together. Leaving Haiti without him was difficult," said Jennifer.

"We returned with the mission's team in March wondering if Judah would remember us," said Jeff. "We didn't have to worry. The minute we arrived, Cindy Lashbrook came out to meet us holding Judah. He recognized me and lunged for Jennifer. We had another great week with Judah and returned to visit him again in June."

The Oettles planned to visit Judah once every three months, but circumstances prevented the September trip. The cancelation of their December trip to Haiti brought more disappointment. The separation from a child they had embraced as a son weighed heavily on the Oettles as they celebrated the arrival of 2010.

Jennifer smiled. "From the very beginning, I prayed all of the paperwork necessary for the adoption would be in the right hands at the right time. But raising the money was a struggle, and the delays compounded my frustration. We finally acquired enough money for Judah's dossier to be filed with the Haitian government. Keith planned to bring the papers to Port-au-Prince on January 17, but he never made it."

On January 12, a catastrophic earthquake rocked the nation of Haiti, killing 200,000; injuring 300,000; and leaving 1,000,000 homeless. The government of Haiti lay in shambles with the Presidential Palace and National Assembly buildings destroyed. The following week, Homeland Security Secretary Janet Napolitano announced a humanitarian parole policy allowing Haitian children in the process of being adopted by American citizens to enter the United States.

Jeff continued the story. "If Keith had succeeded in filing Judah's dossier with the Haitian government, it would have been lost under the rubble created by the earthquake. We would have had no proof Judah was eligible for adoption."

Shortly after the humanitarian policy was announced, the Lashbrooks planned to evacuate the children who were in the process of being adopted. Keith asked Jeff to go to Fort Lauderdale, where a cargo plane would transport him and several other parents to Port-de-Paix to assist in the evacuation. When Jeff arrived at the Fort Lauderdale airport, the concerned adoptive parents were instructed to fly to Santiago in the Dominican Republic. The earliest flight left the following morning and the airport officials refused them entrance into the terminal. They spent a miserable night sleeping on the floor in the baggage claim area.

When they reached Santiago, a relief mission transported them to Port-de-Paix's small dirt landing strip in a five-seat airplane. A United Nations security force escorted the convoy to the mission. "I had not seen Judah since June of 2009. I called his name, wondering if he would remember me. He came running so fast he ran past me and then stopped. He ran back and threw his arms around my leg. It was a moment I'll never forget," said Jeff.

The Lashbrooks chartered a school bus to bring them to Port-au-Prince and to obtain permission to take the children out of the country. Jeff sat on a worn, ripped vinyl seat with Judah on one knee and Donaldson, who a woman in his congregation was adopting, on his other knee.

"The road was so bad I had to wrap my ankles around the braces of the seat in front of me and push my knees into the seat to remain seated. Somehow we made the twelve-hour drive in six. I exited the bus with blisters on both of my knees. I had not had a good night's sleep or bath since I left America three days earlier. We were American citizens with forty-one children and four days of supplies in a city destroyed by an earthquake. The United States Embassy refused to give us refuge."

After numerous phone calls, the order to forbid them entry was rescinded. They were escorted to a waiting room and supplied with a mattress to sleep on the floor. They had access to a bathroom but had no shower and no way to leave.

The man assigned to handle their case left for vacation shortly after they arrived. The flood of misinformation that followed sent their emotions on an unending roller-coaster ride. They were asked to charter a plane and then forbidden to charter a plane. They were told that they would leave that day. An hour later they had to stay another day. They called home with news they would arrive at Fort Lauderdale, then had to call back to report the location changed to Miami, and then called again with the announcement of a new location in Alabama. They ran out of supplies and were eating MREs (meals ready to eat) supplied by the military when a security force arrived to bring them to a C-17 cargo plane destined for Miami.

"It had taken a week, but it seemed like years. When I saw Jeff, he looked like he had just suffered a week of labor pains. I was ready to do it again, but he wanted a break to recuperate." Jennifer laughed. "Now he knows what I went through when I gave birth to our daughters."

I reached to turn off my recorder. Jeff stopped me. He wanted to share his thoughts about adoption. "Adoption is very special to me. I'm the last of six boys. My dad had three boys, and my mother had two when they married. I'm the only child from their union. Jennifer and I had girls. The only way for my line to continue was adoption. Now my namesake will continue through my son. That means a lot to me because God has adopted us."

As I helped the Oettles collect the zoo of balloon animals that my husband had created to entertain the children, Jennifer commented that her family looked odd. Three white girls following their white mother with a Haitian toddler propped on her hip. Jeff securely strapped the children into car seats and found nooks and crannies for the balloons. As they pulled out of the driveway, I pondered a scripture from Revelation: "…[Jesus] purchased men for God from every tribe and language and people and nation" (Revelation 5:9). The Oettle family doesn't look odd. They look like God's family.

Three Powerful Words

When Matt Degier, a missionary with Chi Alpha New Orleans, agreed to tell me about the work God had done in his life, I invited him to my home. I wanted my son, Tim, who was starting college in the fall, to meet Matt, and I thought it would be quiet. Within five minutes of Matt's arrival, Tim walked out the door on his way to work. So much for the beneficial meeting I had envisioned between Matt and Tim. I focused my camera on Matt and pressed record. My dog appeared at the window behind Matt, barking her insistence that I let her back in the house and dashing my hopes for a recording free of unwelcome noise.

Most Christians I've talked to have a defining moment marking when they converted to Christianity. Not so with Matt. Seeped in religion from birth, he "always was" a Christian. He made a commitment to Christ when he was four years old but wasn't sure it registered in God's book of life. He prayed with his father after watching a Billy Graham Crusade when he was ten years old but didn't trust God to guide his life.

"I spent my childhood calculating my batting average with God. I thought God loved me because I was good and knew a lot about the Bible," said Matt. He recalled the time his parents were playing Bible trivia with friends and they were stumped by a question. He overheard their discussion and announced the answer. The ensuing awe and praise that one so young could possess such knowledge established in their minds Matt's destiny to be a minister.

Matt's ideal Christian family life shattered when his parents divorced. He remained with his father, whose badly shaken faith made their church attendance sporadic. Matt continued the motions of Christianity, but his heart drifted far from God. By the time he entered high school, he was addicted to Internet pornography. "I hated myself," said Matt. "I was still the good kid telling people how they needed to serve God, but I had this dark secret that I couldn't tell anyone."

Matt's downward spiral came to the attention of his father. "If you keep pursuing this path," his father warned, "it's not going to end well." Halfway through Matt's sophomore year in high school, his father's counsel registered, and a desire to know God entered Matt's heart. "I wanted to read the Bible, but not as a religious duty. I wanted to pray, but not because I was going to eat or go to bed. For the first time in my life, I wanted to hear from God."

His attendance at a Christian camp the following summer had a profound effect on his life. The teenagers he met resonated with a spiritual reality. Their spirituality was based on a genuine love for God instead of being "a good kid." Realizing his efforts to earn God's favor with a good life were vain, Matt prayed three powerful words: "I give up."

During one of the chapel services at the camp, Matt answered an altar call for anyone who had an addiction. He was so ashamed of his addiction to pornography that he moved to the farthest corner of the altar. "No one prayed for me that night," said Matt. "When I admitted to God that I had a problem, I felt something break within me. The compulsion to sit in front of the Internet for hours viewing pornography left and never returned."

During Matt's junior year in high school, a friend invited him to attend a revival meeting. Before the revival ended, both Matt and his father's lives were transformed by the power of God. His father rededicated his life to Christ. Matt learned the meaning of grace.

"I went to the altar for salvation two, sometimes three, times a week," said Matt. "But I feel like I really got saved sitting in my car in the church parking lot. That is where I accepted grace." Matt had listened to a conversation on Christian radio while driving to church. A man explained how he had accepted Christ, was baptized in water, and then later thought that he wasn't right with God. He kept accepting Christ and getting baptized over and over until someone explained to him that God's grace is sufficient. Matt parked his car in front of the church, rested his forehead on the steering wheel, and wept.

Matt finally understood. He didn't have to make himself "good enough" for God. There is nothing that he could do to add to or to take away from God's grace. For the second time in his life, Matt prayed three powerful words: "I give up." Matt never felt the need to approach the altar for salvation again.

The beneficial meeting I'd planned for my son never materialized. My recording of Matt's story is laced with my dog's howls of protest. All was not lost. Matt taught me the power of surrender. We find liberty to receive a gift that cannot be earned when we "give up."

Teena Myers

Living on the Fringe

Pamela Davis-Noland had twenty-five days to promote her play *The Unacquainted*, a modern-day adaptation of the ministry of Jesus Christ, when we sat down to eat salads at La Madeline's. Months elapsed before I had time to transcribe our conversation and write about her spiritual journey. The unconventional place she entered the kingdom of God began a story of living on the fringe.

"I was a young single mother trying to make a living as a waitress in Lake Charles, Louisiana," said Pamela. "One of my coworkers always talked about Jesus and the love of God. I didn't want her to preach to me, so I eavesdropped on her conversations. My parents and eight siblings were devout Catholics. I'd never heard that we could be forgiven without confessing our sins to a priest or that we could have a personal relationship with God. I was going through a very difficult time, and Michelle always seemed so happy. I wanted to know why, so I asked her to tell me about Jesus. She took me in the bathroom to explain the gospel message, and I prayed for salvation."

Pamela's salvation experience left her on the fringe of her family. She was, according to her mother, the worst of her eight siblings and now a traitor to the Catholic faith. Her parents were not pleased, and her siblings mocked her. Their attitude changed when they saw Pamela's behavior change dramatically. When her parents learned through a friend that Pamela planned to be baptized by immersion, they attended the baptism service. Pamela was surprised and pleased to see them in the congregation. After the service, they prayed to accept Christ as Pamela had but chose to remain in the Catholic Church.

"I ended up helping Michelle as much as she helped me," Pamela continued. "She was amazed how quickly God answered my prayers. Michelle decided she lacked the childlike faith that I found so easy to embrace. The church we attended taught God is a father who loves us, and I believed it. I know if it's something good for me and I ask nicely, God will say yes. If I'm not supposed to have what I ask for, he will say no. I trust God to do what is best for me, and that sums up my walk with God."

Pamela worked at KZWA radio in Lake Charles when the opportunity arose for her to transfer to a larger market at Houston's KHYS and KMJQ. She moved to Houston and later left radio to work as a secretary. "I started writing *Coffee Colored Dreams* before I left Lake Charles. All I wanted to do was write, and I wanted to do something positive. Working an office job left me very dissatisfied," said Pamela.

God fulfilled Pamela's desire to do something positive when she stopped to talk to a woman she often walked by on her way home from work.

"I see you all the time, and I just want to say hi," said Pamela.

"I see you all the time too. My name is Ruth Ollison. I'm the pastor of Beulah Land Community Church. What do you do?"

"I'm a secretary."

"You don't sound like you like it."

"I don't."

Pamela was unemployed the next time she talked to Pastor Ruth and didn't hesitate to accept a job as the pastor's secretary. Her new job led her to the fringe of society in Houston's third ward.

"The third ward was called 'the bottoms' because the people who lived there were at the bottom—uneducated and living in poverty. I took two illiterate teenage brothers into my home. They couldn't go to school because they were taking care of their great-grandmother, who was ill. I helped them care for their grandma and enrolled them in school. I took in many kids that I could not afford to care for, but God always provided. Some are really doing good today and some not so good."

After Pamela's son left for college, she decided to pursue a career in the arts and moved to the city that had become her muse. "Every time I came to New Orleans, I was filled with great ideas. My son was living his own life, and I was single. It was time for me to live my dream. I asked God if he'd take care of me. God said yes, so I moved to New Orleans in 2007. As simple as that may sound, I've not had to work an office job since I moved here. Everything I do now pertains to my art, whether it's promoting my book, producing my plays, working in artist relations at the Essence

Fest, or offering writer's workshops. God said I could do it, and I did."

Pamela signed a contract with SHOP, Inc. (Sweet Hour of Prayer, Inc.) to do five performances of *The Unacquainted* and unexpectedly found herself on the fringe of her own race of people. Pam had hired actors and rehearsed for six weeks when she received a tearful phone call from the woman marketing her play in Henderson, Texas. The play was scheduled to open in two weeks, but they had not sold one ticket. Local pastors were not returning phone calls. Five police cars blocked the entrance to a park frequented by African Americans on the day a rally to promote the play was scheduled. Finally, a local bishop told the marketing director he was receiving an average of thirty calls daily from African American congregations objecting to a black Jesus. SHOP, Inc. pulled the play and refused to honor their contract with Pamela.

"The main character in *The Unacquainted* represents Jesus, and I had cast a black actor," said Pamela. "I was devastated by the creative censorship and heartbroken that it came from my own race of people. My work can be controversial because I'm not afraid to deal with prejudice. In *The Unacquainted*, Pastor Self represents religious people who think they are better than others are. *Coffee Colored Dreams* shines light on prejudice within the African American community toward dark skin. It makes people uncomfortable because it's known that lighter skin is favored, but we don't talk about it. I consider it my ministry to expose prejudice."

I loved Pamela from the moment I met her because she is not afraid to speak her mind. She ultimately found a home for her talents at Fringe Fest New Orleans. Fringe Theater started in Edinburgh, Scotland, in 1947, when the annual arts festival excluded eight performing groups. The excluded performers refused to be denied and found inexpensive or free venues on the fringes of the city. The small group birthed a new festival that grew into the largest arts festival in the world. A perfect fit for someone who boldly exposes the injustice of prejudice.

Like Any Normal Day

"We were established in New Orleans," said Janice McLean. Mark McLean nodded in agreement. "I was an occupational therapist and Mark employed by an international consulting firm. After our daughter's birth, Mark had an opportunity to work in Europe. The new position would enable me to set aside my career and focus on being a mom," said Janice.

"The hardest part of our decision was telling my parents we were moving to Prague with their first grandchild," said Mark.

Mark's new position required him to work in Eastern Europe from Albania to Estonia and to travel extensively in Western Europe. Several years later, when Janice was pregnant with their second daughter, a national position in the United States was available. The McLeans decided to return to America. They relocated to the company's national headquarters in Connecticut.

Tuesday, September 11, 2001, Mark boarded an early train into New York City for a nine o'clock meeting. He took a cab from Grand Central Station to the World Financial Center, where he had been assigned a corner conference room. The building was connected to the Twin Towers by a walkway. Mark walked into the conference room on the thirty-seventh floor and drank in the stunning view of the Hudson River spilling into the Upper New York Bay near the Statue of Liberty. He set his briefcase on the conference table and waited for his coworkers to arrive.

Having used the conference room in the past, he was accustomed to helicopters passing the window on their way to a nearby helipad. When he heard a loud noise, he assumed a helicopter had passed too close to the building. The explosion that rocked the building shortly thereafter could not be ignored.

He walked to the eastside of the building facing the World Trade Center. A massive fire filled his field of vision. He looked down at the crowd gathering in the street. "The crowd reminded me of Mardi Gras—masses of people staring up at passing floats. I wondered why they were standing there. Didn't they know the building could fall on them?" said Mark.

He called corporate headquarters to report his location and see if they needed him to do anything. They were unaware of an emergency. He called Janice, nine months pregnant with their third child.

Janice had put their eldest daughter on the school bus and was preparing their other daughter for Pre-K when the phone rang. At Mark's request, she turned on the TV. There was no "breaking news," and since she was running late, she turned off the TV and grabbed her purse.

Transfixed by the horror unfolding before him, Mark looked out the window again. "That's when I saw a black woman wearing a purple suit falling to her death and then a man in a gray suit. I looked down to see bodies on the street." He returned to the conference room where he had left his briefcase. "As I collected my things, I glanced out the window. An airplane was headed toward me. Suddenly, the plane turned and another explosion rocked the building."

Meanwhile, Janice strapped her daughter into her car seat and then stuck her key into the ignition. As the engine hummed to life, a voice from the radio announced a plane had just hit the World Trade Center. Her cell phone rang. "I just saw a plane hit the World Trade Center," said Mark. "I'm coming home."

Mark grabbed his briefcase. Mary, a member of his team, joined him as he headed for the stairwell already clogged with people from fifty-five floors of the World Financial Center. "I kept thinking either more planes would hit the building or the building would collapse before I could get out," said Mark. The mass of human flesh inched down the stairs. Mark reached for his cell phone and the comfort of his wife's voice. No cell phone service.

Janice walked her daughter into her school like any normal day. "No one knew what was taking place in New York City, and I didn't want to announce the sky is falling without understanding what had happened. It was surreal. I had a doctor's appointment, so I continued my day as usual. It was noon before I returned home and watched the news again. That's when I understood the magnitude of what had happened."

"As I neared the ground floor, I thought about Sodom and Gomorrah and Lot's wife," said Mark. "If I made it out of the building, I wasn't going to let myself look back. I was afraid the horrendous sight would hypnotize me into an immobile trance, sealing my doom."

Forty-five minutes later, Mark and Mary flowed out of the first-floor exit with the river of people seeking safety. He set his face like flint toward the Hudson River, carefully keeping his back to the inferno filling the sky with black smoke. When he reached the river, he turned north toward Grand Central Station. "I was just a few blocks up Westside Highway when the north tower collapsed. I turned. It was horrific. My first thought was tell Janice 'I'm Okay' but the cell phone was useless."

Mark spotted an attendant in a parking lot and asked to use the landline phone. Comforted by Janice's calm assurance that everything would be okay, he exited the lot into mayhem. Emergency vehicles sped south toward the Twin Towers. More emergency vehicles sped north with dented roofs and broken windows. People gathered around car radios and shouted the radio announcer's instructions to people fleeing from the terrorist attack. "Don't go near the Empire State Building. It will be hit next," someone shouted. Mark looked up. He was standing near the Empire State Building.

He stopped at an ATM hoping to withdraw enough cash to pay for a ride out of the hell surrounding him. His search for a car with a Connecticut license plate proved futile. Fifty blocks later, Mark and Mary reached Grand Central Station. The station had closed until threats of an attack on the station could be investigated. With no way to leave, Mary's room in a nearby hotel served as a refuge. "I caught a train home after the station reopened. When I arrived, Janice had dinner ready like any normal evening," said Mark.

I asked Mark and Janice if the experience shook their faith in God. They answered with a resounding no. They attributed the peace they experienced that day to the Christian faith instilled in them by their godly parents.

The spiritual heritage Mark and Janice received from their parents guided them safely through a tragic day in our nation's history, but their experience is not unique. Stories abound of divine intervention that kept people safe or out of harm's way on the day of the attack. Clearly, there are benefits to making the Most High our dwelling place.

Looking for Love

Tasha met me for lunch. When the food arrived, she prayed, "Lord, thank you for this food and fellowship. Guide me to say the right things so others will be blessed." I pressed record and listened to a sordid story of molestation, physical abuse, and abortion. Several times I queried, "Do you want that public?" Tasha assured me I could share everything that she told me. She wanted to give hope to women who are suffering as she had.

Tasha's parents fought often. Her father believed a woman should be completely dependent on her husband. To keep his wife from going to school, he put broken glass in his son's crib. "My mother tried to shoot him," said Tasha. "I wanted her to kill him. She didn't know he had been molesting me since I was three years old."

Tasha cut her wrist at ten years of age. Her mother brought her to several different churches seeking help. Tasha went to the altar at a Pentecostal church, where she prayed for salvation. But her mother never committed her life to Christ, and Tasha received little support in living a Christian life.

Tasha paused to reflect on her experience at the Pentecostal church. "Giving my heart to the Lord at age eleven was for the long road ahead of me. I'd be burning in hell right now if I hadn't done so."

Severely depressed, Tasha's mother attempted suicide. Her father took his four children to live with their grandmother while their mother recuperated in the hospital. Tasha's mother filed for divorce after she was released from the hospital, and Tasha did not see her again for a long time. Free from her husband's control, Tasha's mother became a nurse and then remarried Tasha's father. One morning Tasha awoke to find her father in bed with her. She complained to her mother, who ignored her plea for help. Tasha turned to drugs to escape the harsh reality of her life.

"My mother didn't know how to help me, so she sent me to mental hospitals. The treatment became a game to me. I knew how to act so they would give me medicine. When the insurance ran out, I escaped from the hospital, lived in Iowa, and then went to Arkansas. Finally, I called my mom for a bus ticket home. The police picked me up and brought me back to the hospital. The psychiatrist diagnosed me as manic-depressive, prescribed medicine, and discharged me."

Tasha returned home no better than when she left. Her mother gave her $500 and told her to leave. She used the money to return to Iowa with her boyfriend and became pregnant. Tasha's family pressured her to marry the baby's father. The marriage ended four months after she gave birth to their daughter.

When Tasha became pregnant by a new boyfriend, her mother insisted she have an abortion. Tasha refused. "The fetus is just a blob of tissue," said her mother and dropped Tasha off at the abortion clinic. Tasha felt troubled the moment she stepped out of the car. "The clinic told me if people were picketing to look at the ground and walk straight in. I wish someone had been picketing that day because I would not have gone inside."

Tasha's chin quivered as tears filled her eyes. "While they were doing the abortion, I looked up. I don't know why. I just looked up and saw tiny bones. Everyone had lied to me. It wasn't a blob of tissue. My baby was being torn apart. I wanted to stop, but it was too late."

I stopped my recorder and touched Tasha's trembling hand. "We don't have to talk about this."

"No," said Tasha. "It's all right. I never want to have such a hard heart that I don't weep. I know God allowed me to see the truth." She wiped the tears from her eyes and continued her story.

Tasha returned home in physical and emotional pain. She tried to drown the image of her baby's mutilated body in a sea of drugs. Angry that Tasha had aborted their baby, her boyfriend became physically abusive. "I ended our relationship, and I just went wild," said Tasha. "One morning I awoke from a drunken stupor and realized I had been raped."

Seeking an escape from the out-of-control whirlwind her life had become, she called her father and threatened suicide if he didn't send her a plane ticket to join him in Alaska. Six weeks after joining her father, Tasha discovered that she was pregnant again. Unwilling to bear the child of the man who raped her, she felt justified in having another abortion.

Tasha returned to New Orleans, where she met and then married Jonathan. He was different from the men she usually dated. He showered her with presents and surprised her with flowers. After Tasha gave birth to their son, she fell into a postpartum depression. She left her children in the care of family members and traded some jewelry for 500 Valiums. "I went to my mother's house, took all of the Valium, and then lay down to die. Several hours later, a friend woke me. I was so angry that I wasn't dead; I stayed high for two weeks."

When Tasha descended from the two-week high, she confronted her mother about the abusive way she had been raised. Her mother had little sympathy. Wounded by her mother's callous attitude and disappointed by her failed suicide, Tasha grabbed her mother's car keys and drove to a nearby Walmart. The car idled in the parking lot as she contemplated driving through the store. Then a light post caught her eye. She placed a heavy foot on the gas. As the car gained momentum, she prayed, "God, take me now. I just want to be with you." The force of the impact pushed the engine into her lap.

Tasha slipped in and out of consciousness. Fear on the medics faces. Darkness. A policeman writing a ticket suddenly stopped when he saw her. Darkness. Sirens wailing. Muffled voices. More darkness. Medics wheeled her into the emergency room. The shocked look on the doctors' faces scared Tasha. Before she lost consciousness again, she heard, "Your daughter will be dead by the end of the week."

Thirty days later, Tasha awoke from a coma to learn that she had crushed every bone in her foot, cracked her pelvis, lost all of her teeth, and nearly severed her arm. After months of reconstructive surgery, she was discharged, wearing a cast on her left arm and right leg. Jonathan picked her up from the hospital, berated her about the bill, and then left her at her mother's house.

"My mother ignored me. My brothers stole my medicine. I couldn't open a can of soup to eat. I couldn't bathe myself. I remember sitting in my wheelchair crying. One of my brothers finally wheeled me outside and washed my filthy hair with the garden hose. I don't know what I would have done if my aunt had not taken me into her home."

Tasha's aunt taught her about God and brought her to church. A guest speaker shared how God had brought him to heaven. Tasha knew what the speaker would say before he said it. Her mind free from the fog of drugs, a precious memory came rushing back.

"I visited heaven when I was in the coma. I remembered a river. Everything was green and bright, but there were no shadows. Someone walked by my side. I guess he was an angel. He told me I was in heaven, where there is no darkness. That's why I didn't see shadows. Then he gave me a piece of fruit. I bit into the fruit and juice dripped down my chin. A line of people dressed in white passed us as we walked toward a gate with names carved in stone. We walked through the gate, and I stepped onto a street made of gold. I saw God. He wore a hooded robe with light shining from the openings. The moment I saw him, it felt like all the bones left my body, and I collapsed on my face.

"When I looked up, Jesus stepped out of God and extended his arms to me. The third time he extended his arms, I was instantly at his feet. I saw the holes from his crucifixion. An overwhelming sorrow swept over me, and I wept. Suddenly, I was sitting on God's lap. His face looked like fixtures of light. We talked, but not with words—an exchange of thoughts. God cried and told me how much he loved me, how he had always been there and never left me."

Once again, Tasha could no longer contain her emotion as she told her story. I sat in solemn silence until she regained her composure.

"There are no words to describe what I felt. After remembering that experience, I changed. In the past, I cried all the time. God must have healed something in me, because I stopped crying. Even when I felt like crying, I couldn't."

Jonathan divorced Tasha. She was pregnant from another failed relationship when she met Paul. "The night I met Paul, he had just come from church, where he had prayed for salvation. I told him I was giving up my baby for adoption. We married and joined a church. This time I was determined to obey God."

A month into her marriage, Tasha discovered she had married a drunk and a wife beater. Her marriage problems and lack of maternal feelings for the child she bore made it easy for her to sign the adoption papers.

"After I gave my baby up for adoption, I became pregnant by Paul. We named our son Brian. My marriage was seven years of hell that broke my pride. I guess God had to give me someone really rotten so I could see the rottenness in me. I fasted, prayed, and learned to lean on God for everything."

As Tasha grew closer to God, Paul became distant and stopped attending church. When he started watching pornography, she grew concerned about the safety of her daughters. She wanted to divorce Paul but had no means to support herself and her children.

As Tasha fretted over her future, three-year-old Brian walked into the room and sang, "God is in control and will not let his children be forsaken. Don't worry; now is not the time to worry." Encouraged by her son's impromptu admonition, Tasha prayed and fasted forty days for God to heal her marriage.

Paul enrolled in Teen Challenge, a drug rehabilitation program. While he was away, Tasha's pastor paid for her to attend a retreat where she could seek God and receive professional counseling. Before she left for the retreat, she warned Paul if he quit the Teen Challenge program or sold one thing in their house to buy drugs, their marriage was over. In the middle of the retreat, Paul called to confess he had gone on a binge but was returning to Teen Challenge. Tasha left the retreat early, fearful that he had sold everything they owned. Her fears were confirmed when she walked into their empty home.

Tasha moved into a cheap motel and found work at a dry cleaner in a nearby strip mall. She was flipping through the tags on the clothes when she saw the name Shanks. She wondered if it was the same Pastor Bill Shanks she had met briefly at an abortion protest. Later that day, a man walked into the dry cleaners to pick up his clothes.

"Shanks," he said.

"Like shanking in a prison," Tasha replied, and then looked up. "Are you a pastor?"

Pastor Shanks smiled broadly and nodded.

"Can I come to your church?"

"Sure," he replied.

"I don't have a car."

"I'll pick you up."

"I felt healing just standing next to Pastor Shanks. At times I could barely walk when I was near him. God used him to repair the damaged image I had of a father figure. Sometimes he would hug me and I'd tense up, thinking something sexual would follow. He made time to talk to me and listened when I talked like I had something important to say. He gave me the father's love I'd looked for all of my life, and it made me feel whole."

There is a chorus we often sang in children's church: "Heaven is a wonderful place/Filled with Glory and Grace/I want to see my Savior's face/Heaven is a wonderful place." Few people are privileged to experience heaven and live to tell about it as Tasha did, but it wasn't her trip to heaven that changed her life. Finding the love of a father made her shattered life whole again.

make me ordinary

I sat transfixed as Pamela Harrleson recounted her struggle with weight loss and the evolution of her book, *The Rest of the Truth*. She dropped tidbits of the remarkable transformation God performed in her life before she developed a weight problem, which whetted my appetite to know more. At the conclusion of her presentation, she agreed to meet me for lunch.

"I came from a good family who was well-known in the community. My father was the president of the Downtown Merchants Association, and my mother was a homemaker. Every Sunday they brought us to services at the United Methodist Church. I was loved, which leaves me at a loss to explain my abnormal behavior," said Pam.

Despite her loving family, Pam became obsessive, compulsive, and uncontrollable at a young age. Her personality flaws were over and above the normal quirks of others: a tendency to isolate herself, poor eye contact, an inability to listen and to communicate, stealing, and lying. When she was seven, she packed a wagon with supplies, wrote a note that she was leaving, and then hid in a ditch until her parents found her. Eating disorders began at age eight. She tried to commit suicide at age eleven by slitting her wrists with a razor blade.

Pam paused to sip her iced tea and then continued her story. "The second time I ran away from home, a friend from school let me live in her attic until she saw my face in the newspaper and on TV. Forced to leave and having no place to go, I called home, and the police picked me up. Then I stole my parents' car. They found me at a motel in bed with a drunken old man. By this time my parents were sure I had a mental problem."

"My parents committed me to a state-run mental health hospital. I avoided the rats by sleeping in a chair." Pam pointed to her head. "My thoughts were dark and distorted. I liked the hospital and was disappointed when they released me six weeks later."

Concerned about the stigma Pam bore for being a patient in a mental hospital, her parents enrolled her in a private boarding school run by the Seventh Day Adventists. Pam smiled. "My parents loved me and gave me a wonderful opportunity to turn my life around." Her smile faded. "I snuck out one night and was picked up by two men. After partying all night, the men took me back to the school and left me in a drunken stupor on the lawn. My parents' hopes that I would graduate and live a normal life were dashed when the school called and demanded them to come get me."

A judge sentenced Pam to the Columbia State Training School. Most of the girls at the reform school were poor and from abusive homes. They relieved their frustrations by beating up new girls when they entered the bathroom. Pam learned most of the girls were illiterate and won their favor by reading their letters from social workers. Life in the reform school became bearable when she befriended a large girl who became her bodyguard.

"The girls at the reform school scared me straight," said Pam. "I wanted God and asked to meet the chaplain. If he had told me God loved me and could help me, I think I would have responded. Instead, he told me how good my parents were and how they did not deserve the pain my actions created."

When Pam returned home, her parents allowed her to date a young man from a nearby naval base, hoping a husband would normalize her life. "Everyone loved Al, but he was overweight. At the time, I was thin. I think he was happy to have a cute girlfriend and didn't pay attention to my mental problems. I felt nothing for Al. When he asked me to marry him, I said yes, but I don't know why."

Pam decided to improve her life while Al was in Vietnam and enrolled in college. She quickly fell into an immoral lifestyle. Distressed that she could not control herself, she attempted suicide. Her parents admitted her to a private psychiatric hospital. Electric shock treatments failed to change her behavior. "When Al returned from Vietnam and learned what I had done, he still wanted me. No one should have wanted me, but he loved me very much and saw the good in me."

At this point in her story, Pam stopped to reflect on her religious experience. "Many people had the opportunity to share the gospel with me, but I don't remember anyone telling me that God loved me and could help me. Plenty of people scolded me for my bad behavior and demanded to know why I did things that hurt my parents and husband. The burden for my behavior was always placed on my shoulders, but I didn't know how to change."

Hoping a different environment would help Pam, Al took his young bride to South Carolina, where Susan, Al's sister-in-law, talked to Pam about biblical prophecy and gave her a Bible written in modern-day English. Pam believed the gospel story was a myth, but the prophecies that Jesus's life fulfilled intrigued her.

When Pam's behavior showed no signs of improvement, Al expressed regret for marrying her. Pam fell into a depression. Thoughts of suicide returned. For the first time in her life, Pam wanted help. She committed herself to a mental hospital, desperate to find a cure.

"I looked out the window of the hospital and watched a mother put her children in the car as she chatted with a neighbor. I remember thinking, *She is ordinary, but I'll never be ordinary*." Having lost hope of living a normal life and weary of hurting the people who loved her, Pam escaped from the hospital. She planned to hitchhike to New Orleans and disappear among the street people.

Pam leaned forward, her voice serious. "As I walked down a dark and lonely road, I thought about the prophecies Jesus had fulfilled and about the prophecies in the Middle East, which had recently been fulfilled. I remembered some scriptures I had read and thought about the Billy Graham Crusades I had watched with my parents, which always concluded with an invitation to come just as you are. Then I remembered a sermon about faith I'd heard as a child. The pastor said all we needed was faith the size of a tiny mustard seed. Those thoughts gave me permission to call on God, so I prayed, 'God I still have a lot of questions and doubts, but I think I have a little faith, and I want you.'" Pam's voice trembled, tears rolled down her cheeks as she continued her story. "I pleaded with God to make me ordinary."

Pam wiped away the tears. "After I prayed, I looked around and realized I was alone on a dark highway near a forest. I knew God had done something in my mind because I reacted like an ordinary person would. I was afraid. In the past, I always ran away from problems. For the first time in my life, I had the strength to face the consequences of my actions. As I walked back toward the hospital, I prayed for a safe ride. A nice man in a station wagon stopped. When I got in the car, the fear left. He brought me back to the hospital."

The next day, Pam felt drawn to the Bible. She spent every spare moment reading scriptures. One day she awoke, and everything looked different. "The air was different. The room looked different, and I felt like I was a different person. Eventually, my husband noticed the dramatic change in me. He confessed that he had accepted Christ when he was twelve but had drifted away."

Pam and Al returned to church, but the road wasn't easy. The first fifteen years of their marriage were difficult as Al taught Pam normal social skills. The last fifteen years, both of them developed severe obesity problems. Pam eventually won her battle with obesity and became a personal fitness trainer. After years on the dieting rollercoaster and multiple bariatric surgeries, Al lost his battle. He died of obesity-related illnesses.

The Apostle Paul wrote to the Corinthians, "[Love] always protects, always trusts, always hopes, always perseveres. Love never fails." I turned off my recorder and studied the face of a woman transformed by the love of God and a husband who never gave up on her. She is the most ordinary person I have ever met.

Between the First and Second Pew

I was disappointed when I could not attend the Louisiana State Women's Ministry Convention. I'd hoped to write Rhonda Rock's testimony. Sonya McLean, Director of Women's Ministry Unlimited, told me not to fret. Rhonda was scheduled to speak at our church the following Sunday. I sat in Hosanna's conference room with Rhonda and listened to a powerful story of endurance, overcoming bitterness, and healing.

Rhonda was the daughter of a Pentecostal preacher. Her family moved from city to city as her father ministered to small struggling churches. When the church stabilized, he moved to another church in crisis. In between pastorates, he worked as an evangelist and the family lived in Claremore, Oklahoma, where Rhonda was born.

Rhonda's family encountered the most difficult pastorate of her father's ministry when she was nine years old. "My parents dealt with a lot of stress, and I felt the hurt in their lives. One Sunday night, my dad preached a message about drawing closer to God. A sweet spirit filled the church as we began to pray. I needed something more in my life, so I knelt down between the first and second pew and asked the Lord to come near me. The next thing I knew, I was speaking in tongues," a smiling Rhonda said as she fondly recalled her experience. "I knew something powerful and life-changing had happened to me that night. Not only did I need the power of God, my mother needed to know God was with them. If my mom were here, she would tell you that my baptism in the Holy Spirit was the redemption of being in that difficult pastorate."

Rhonda's family returned to Claremore during her senior year of high school. "I met Larry Rock that year. We dated for two years. When God confirmed Larry was his choice for me, I married him. God knew I needed a rock, and not just as a last name. Our first twelve years were a long, difficult road."

A few months after they married, Larry rushed Rhonda to the emergency room for hemorrhaging. Four hours of surgery later, the doctors found the source of the bleeding. When Rhonda awoke in recovery, the doctor said to her, "You have two uteruses, and they are full of tumors the size of grapefruits. As soon as you are strong enough, I'll schedule you for a radical hysterectomy."

"Larry and I felt children were a blessing from the Lord and refused to be denied this blessing. We prayed, and I took a step of faith. I told the doctors to remove the tumors but leave everything necessary for me to have children. Three surgeries later, he had removed all the tumors, but he didn't know which uterus was functioning. He insisted I have a hysterectomy. I argued with him, and he gave me three months to get pregnant."

Within three months, Rhonda was pregnant. She endured a difficult, painful pregnancy carrying her baby on the side, like a football, where the baby had little room to grow. Nine months later, the doctors removed more tumor than baby, but Rhonda and Larry had a beautiful, healthy baby girl. Once again, the doctor insisted Rhonda have a hysterectomy.

"I knew I was pushing it when I refused. I had one miracle, and my faith was strong. I had two more surgeries to remove tumors and gave birth to my son in 1980. This time I agreed to have the hysterectomy, but my body was wrecked. The multiple surgeries and difficult pregnancies had compromised my immune system."

The doctor put Rhonda on a regiment of hormone shots and medication to stabilize her body. She could not tolerate the sun, had difficulty breathing, and developed severe food allergies and acute food intolerance. Potatoes gave her migraine headaches that lasted for days. Bananas caused her throat to swell. As soon as she mastered how to eat, new allergies developed until she was allergic to thirty-nine foods, leaving her very little to eat.

"I believe God heals. The doctors told me I would never have children, and I had two miracles. I asked God to heal me many times. Six years later, I weighed eighty-nine pounds and contemplated suicide. When you seek God for something and it doesn't happen on your timetable, it's easy to stop trusting God. I felt abandoned and believed the lie that God didn't love me."

One night Rhonda slipped out of bed to take a sleeping pill. She filled a glass with water and set it on the kitchen table. She twisted the top off the bottle containing the pills and heard, "Don't take one, take two; you will sleep better. Rhonda took two pills from the bottle. "Why not take all of them? Then you won't feel anything anymore." Rhonda poured the pills onto the table in a little heap and then reached for the bottle of pain pills. She emptied those pills on top of the sleeping pills and then proceeded to open every bottle of medication the doctors had prescribed.

"I don't know how long I sat looking at that mountain of pills before I scooped up the pills in one hand and grabbed the glass of water with the other. My hands were shaking so bad I dropped the glass. It shattered. I was in a spiritual battle. My thoughts out of control," said Rhonda.

Rhonda stared at the shattered glass. "It's okay," the tormenting voice whispered, "there are other ways to kill yourself. Pick up a shard of glass and cut your wrists."

Rhonda reached for a shard. This time she heard the comforting voice of the Holy Spirit cutting through her depression. "The enemy comes to kill, steal, and destroy. I have come that you might have life. Is this the way you want to die, Rhonda?" Questions flashed in Rhonda's mind. *Do you want the children you prayed for to find your lifeless body lying in a pool of blood? Do you want the husband God gave you to raise your children alone? Is this the legacy you want to leave your family?*

"God's voice returned me to a place of sanity. I thanked God for intervening and decided to live for my children and husband, whether he healed me or not. I set my shoulder to the plow and endured another six years."

In 1997, news of a revival in Pensacola, Florida, reached Oklahoma. Stories of salvation, healings, and deliverance abounded. Rhonda's church chartered a bus to attend the revival, but she wasn't interested. She had made peace with her lot in life, and it no longer mattered if God healed her.

"I was still mad at God. My husband forced me to go to the revival. We watched fourteen hours of videos on the way to Pensacola. People all around me were being blessed, and that made me even madder. We arrived to stand in the hot Florida sun for hours. Then it rained. I was hot and sticky, then soaked and seething with anger by the time the church doors opened. Hundreds of people lurched forward, anxious to be included in the main sanctuary. Larry and I were the last two allowed in before they diverted the crowds to another building to watch the service by video. The only seating left in the sanctuary was in the deaf section, and we could only sit there if I interpreted for the deaf."

Rhonda felt empty inside but recognized the heavy presence of God's Spirit fill the building as she signed "Draw Me Close" written by Kelly Carpenter. Halfway through the song, Rhonda was shaking so bad another interpreter replaced her. Rhonda stood between the first and second pew—the same place she asked God to draw close to her when she was nine years old.

"Larry told me I looked like a rag doll that God shook and then dropped on the floor. I lay on the floor, aware of everything going on around me but unable to move. I heard God say, 'You are full of anger, bitterness, and unforgiveness.' Then I saw the last twelve years of my life like a movie. Every time I watched my family eat, and I could not. Every time I went to the bathroom and cried. Every time I cursed because I did not have the life I wanted. Then God said, 'If you repent, I'll forgive you and heal your body.'"

The moment Rhonda cried out in repentance, the shaking stopped. Warmth traveled like liquid heat throughout every part of her body. Four hours later, she stood to her feet, transformed by the presence of God. She felt like the little girl who had asked God to draw close when she was nine years old. The following morning, Rhonda ate pancakes for breakfast with no adverse effects but didn't tell anyone that God had healed her.

"When Larry and I arrived home, I asked him to buy me a double cheeseburger from Sonic. He looked at me like I was speaking a foreign language, but he bought me one and prayed over it before we ate. I dived into that hamburger. When I looked up, Larry was crying. He said, 'You've been healed, haven't you?' That was fourteen years ago, and I haven't had one physical reaction to food since the day God drew me close to him again."

The Star Maker

When I learned Billy Graham's grandson, Will Graham, would speak at the Katrina Anniversary Prayer Rally hosted by First Baptist New Orleans, I called Dr. David Crosby for permission to photograph the service. During our conversation, he gave me permission to copy material from his website to post on NOLA's faith blog, and I requested to write about his ministry.

After hearing David's story, I had to reevaluate what "knowledge puffs up" means (1 Corinthians 8:1). He is a busy pastor of a large church, yet he not only made time in his schedule for me; he sought to give me as much time as I desired. His bachelor of arts, master of divinity, and doctorate of religion failed to puff. David dripped with humility and gushed with compassion for the poor.

At the tender age of seven, David experienced a deep sense of being lost. He approached his father to share his fear of spending an eternity without God. "I really want to have Christ in my life and know that I am saved," David told his father. His father led him to commit his life to Christ. That experience became a defining moment that set the course of David's life.

Four years later, David's father accepted the pastorate at a church in Texas, and David's ministry began. Eleven-year-old David and three of his eight brothers formed a quartet and sang at a rescue mission in

El Paso. He recalled with fondness praying with the men who came to the altar after his father preached and then joining them for a meal after the service. David assumed the leadership of the quartet when he was seventeen. Before the Crosby Brothers quartet disbanded, they traveled to three hundred churches in eleven states, sang on two weekly radio programs, and made four albums.

His family moved to central Texas so his father could pursue a degree at Howard Payne University. While studying at the university, David's father accepted the pastorate at a Baptist church. "There are two reasons my family became Baptist. My father had good rapport with the Baptist church, and he wanted his children to attend accredited schools," said David.

David enrolled in Baylor University to study journalism. In the middle of his freshman year, he suffered a crisis of faith. He had always studied the Bible from a devotional point of view. The religion classes he took approached the Bible from a scholarly point of view. One of his professors believed in Darwin's theory of evolution, leaving David confused and frustrated.

His professors shook his faith, but the solid foundation of Christ proved stronger than the wisdom of man. "The night I asked God what to do," said David, "'Jesus is all you need' rumbled out of my soul. From that point on, I became both intellectually and spiritually a Jesus person. I knew that God had called me to preach, so I changed my major to religion."

After David graduated, he served as senior pastor in various churches. During his pastorate at Trinity Baptist

Church, he met the infamous pickax murderer Karla Faye Tucker. Karla had accepted Christ six months after her arrest while incarcerated in Houston's Harris County Jail. David baptized Karla in the Mountain View Prison while she awaited execution.

Tucker's appeal to commute her death sentence to life imprisonment drew support from world figures Waly Bacre Ndiaye, the United Nations commissioner on summary and arbitrary executions; the World Council of Churches; Pope John Paul II; and Italian Prime Minister Romano Prodi. Pat Robertson, founder of CBN, delighted death penalty opponents when he called for clemency.

Shortly after Tucker's execution, David told the Baptist Press that Karla exemplified the love of God as well as any one he had ever known. He also reevaluated his position on capital punishment. His relationship with Karla put a face on the death penalty and made him question if society can implement capital punishment equitably.

David had purchased forty-one acres and built a house for his family in Texas. He loved his ministry, his new home, and walking outside at night to look at the stars. When a committee from New Orleans contacted him about a church on St. Charles Avenue, he wasn't interested.

The committee called a second time. Confident his wife would not be interested in moving, he discussed the offer with her. During a time of prayer, the Lord impressed on his wife's heart that they should talk to the committee. David traveled to New Orleans in 1996 intent on doing little more than talking.

He met with the committee and returned to his eleventh-floor hotel room for a restless night. Around 4:00 a.m., he walked onto the balcony and looked up to see the stars. "The stars at night are big and bright deep in the heart of Texas," said David, "but they were not so bright deep in the heart of New Orleans."

Dismayed, David exclaimed, "God, where are the stars?" A twinkle caught his eye, and he looked down. The city dotted with a sea of man-made lights sprawled awkwardly around the river. As he pondered what he should do about the committee's offer, he heard a voice as clear as though someone spoke audibly. "The people in the city are your stars now. I want you to come to New Orleans and help people 'shine like stars in the universe'" (Philippians 2:15).

David smiled broadly. "That is my calling. I've been here longer than any other place, and I don't plan on leaving." Since David accepted the pastorate at First Baptist New Orleans, he has led his congregation to put their faith into action by practicing Jesus's command to love your neighbor as yourself.

In 2004, he heard Mayor Ray Nagin say, "The single most important factor to permanently lift a family out of poverty is home ownership." Intrigued, David contacted the Department of Housing and Urban Development (HUD) and the New Orleans Redevelopment Authority (NORA) to verify the statement made by Mayor Nagin. Both HUD and NORA confirmed that home ownership permanently changes the economic future of a family.

David immediately founded the Baptist Crossroads Project and partnered with Habitat for Humanity to build forty single-family dwellings. Plans were delayed by Hurricane Katrina but not forgotten. In 2006, the Baptist Crossroads Project built sixty homes for the displaced citizens of the Ninth Ward.

I've heard many stories about people salvaged from the depths of sin by Jesus's grace. No one had the profound effect on me that David Crosby did. The greatest story of all is a selfless life spent in service to others. From the young boy who prayed with derelicts to the man who baptized Karla Faye Tucker to his quest of permanently lifting the poor out of poverty, David has consistently extended a hand of hope to the hopeless. There are few people better equipped than David Crosby to make God's people shine like stars.

Hazard's Journey

I pulled into Hosanna's parking lot in a monsoon. Patrick Hazard agreed to meet me in the youth house. There were two houses on the property. I'd forgotten to ask which house belonged to the youth. Fortunately, he arrived shortly after I did, and we splashed our way into the youth house.

Pat gave his life to the Lord at the tender age of five. Misguided Christians taught Pat that life would be wonderful if he served God. Reality shook his faith when his third-grade teacher had him suspended for preaching the gospel in school. Throughout his childhood, he attended church camps, which renewed his zeal, but the blaze quickly flickered into a smoldering ember.

The theology Pat embraced shattered when his parents divorced. Disillusioned by the teaching he accepted as truth, Pat abandoned his faith to pursue a life of crime. He left home at age fifteen and survived on the streets of New York dealing drugs and sleeping on park benches. Two years later, a judge gave Pat an ultimatum: join the army or go to jail.

Before Pat left for boot camp, a friend asked him a simple Bible question. "I don't remember the question," said Pat, "but I remember feeling sorry for him. My friend came from a wealthy family. He had everything he wanted in life, but he was so miserable that he wanted to commit suicide." Pat searched the Bible to find answers for his friend. Instead, he found the truth. The Christians he read about were persecuted, imprisoned, and some died for their faith. Pat closed his Bible with the realization that his early instruction in Christianity was wrong.

He hoped a military career would give him a fresh start, and he resolved to abandon drugs. Drugs refused to abandon him. While stationed on an army base in Louisiana, he discovered pushers were scamming unsuspecting recruits by drying leaves and stems, adding seeds, and spraying the fake weed with roach killer. "I helped the recruits find the good stuff," said Pat. Pat's activities were discovered, and he soon found himself in jeopardy of being kicked out of the army.

A compassionate sergeant kept Pat from a dishonorable discharge by building on the one thing Pat could do well: run. He assigned Pat to teach the men in his platoon how to run better. Pat quickly improved their running scores. Discovering his natural ability to teach redeemed Pat and set his feet on a new path.

"I was aware of a void in my life when I met Yulanda," said Pat. "Her parents invited me to attend church with them. My relationship with Yulanda wasn't working, so I decided to break up with her by embarrassing her family during a church service."

Pat mocked the congregation, which patiently endured his antics. Then he spoke profanity loud enough for the pastor to hear as he preached his message. When Pat saw the pastor walking toward him after the service, he was positive the pastor would ban him from attending the church. Instead, the pastor gave him a warm handshake and invited him to attend their Thursday night prayer meeting. Disarmed by the love expressed toward him, Pat accepted the invitation.

He arrived with Yulanda's family, expecting the kind of prayer meetings he attended as a child: fifteen minutes of prayer followed by socializing. Two hours later, the people were still praying. Bored and ready to leave, Pat started an argument with Yulanda. Her father intervened and challenged Pat to consider his life.

Pat walked to the back of the church and sat down. He thought about the constant trouble in which he found himself and admitted that he wasn't happy. He studied the people in the church. The emotion the people expressed as they prayed contradicted his belief that God no longer speaks. He wanted the kind of relationship with God they had.

In a moment of honesty, Pat told God he would read the Bible and pray but he wasn't going to change. He didn't want another stint in the white-washed walls of a church. Pat kept his commitment, and God did what Pat couldn't. He turned Pat's love for drugs and alcohol into disgust. Instead of breaking up with Yulanda, he married her.

Shortly after they married, the army sent Pat on his first hostile-fire tour in Haiti. While his combat buddies sought to escape their misery on the army-imposed two-beer limit per week, Pat read his Bible. He also met Sergeant Woodson, a devout Christian. He taught Pat how to study the Bible, to preach, and to design worship services around the Word of God. "I wasn't easy to work with," said Pat, "but Sergeant

Woodson had a philosophy: 'I'm willing to make you mad now to save you later.'"

Pat completed the Haitian tour and received orders that sent him to Bosnia, where he met Sergeant Cahill. "Cahill was a walking Bible who taught me how to analyze scripture," said Pat. The year-long tour in Bosnia had been difficult on his family. He declined reenlistment and accepted a job as an ironworker. The company immediately sent him to Slidell, Louisiana, to rebuild a high school destroyed by Hurricane Katrina. Over the next forty days, he had a similar conversation with a young coworker.

"I vividly remember the last time we had the conversation," said Pat. The young man said, "Hazard, I'm twenty-three. I have fifty years before I need to think about that church stuff."

"You're not guaranteed to make it home after work," Pat replied.

"I'm a good person."

"If you are judged for the good you have done, you'll also be judged for the bad you have done, and any bad at all will disqualify you from heaven."

"If everyone fails, how can anyone go to heaven?"

"By choosing Christ as your judge, confessing him as Lord, and receiving the gift of salvation he has freely provided," Pat replied. This time the young man received Pat's message and prayed for salvation. They agreed to meet early the next morning for coffee and donuts. "He never made it," said Pat. "On his way to meet me, he was killed in an automobile accident."

Pat reminded me of my sister. Both were caught in a web of false doctrine that led them astray. The Bible warns us that there will be false teachers in our day just as there were false prophets in the nation of Israel. While the truth is not always found in the mouth of religious leaders, it can always be found in the pages of the Bible.

Wait on the Lord

The first time I saw Dr. Joe Neal McKeever, he was sketching two young women. At the time, he held the position of Director of Missions for the Baptist Association for Greater New Orleans. Joe (he insisted I call him "Joe") graciously consented to contribute his blog articles to NOLA's faith blog. I made a mental note to contact Joe and request permission to write about his ministry. The note hung on the corkboard in my mind for months before I stumbled across him on Facebook. Three months later, I found time to buy him a hot chocolate at Café du Monde. He arrived with sketchpad in hand.

Joe entered the world in 1940 near Nauvoo, Alabama. As far back as he could remember, church had been a part of his life. His first six years revolved around activities at the New Oak Grove Free Will Baptist Church.

His father relocated the family to the mountainous coal fields of West Virginia when Joe was seven years old, and they joined a Methodist Church. "The church was wonderful," said Joe, "a great place for a child. I loved the Lord, loved the church, and loved the pastor."

The following year, Joe sat beside his mother when the pastor gave an altar call for salvation. Joe looked up at his mother. "Can I go to the altar?" She nodded her approval. He slipped out of his seat and walked to the front of the church. The pastor shook Joe's hand

and instructed him to kneel down while he waited for others to join them. Several children joined Joe at the altar before the pastor instructed them to stand, and he introduced them as new converts. Joe smiled. "The following Sunday they gave us grape juice and crackers for our first communion, but no one explained anything to us. We were 'in,' but nothing changed in my life."

Three years later, Joe's family returned to Alabama and the New Oak Grove Free Will Baptist Church. When Joe was eleven years old, an evangelist came to the church for a two-week revival. Thoroughly convinced of Jesus's soon return, the evangelist declared he would still be driving his 1948 Pontiac when Jesus comes back.

"I wonder if he's still driving that car." Joe laughed. "When he gave the altar call, I had an overwhelming sense of guilt and a burden about my own condition. In those days, congregation members followed you to the altar. By the time I reached the altar, there were eight people with me. I didn't know how to pray, so I just knelt and cried. I still remember my aunt whispering in my ear, 'You never were a bad boy, Joe Neal. You just weren't saved.' I don't think I said anything to God, but I knew something had changed. I walked back to my seat with an overwhelming sense of love for everyone in the church."

Joe graduated from high school intent on becoming a college history professor. While pursuing his dream at Berry College, his sister called requesting his assistance while her husband was away on business. Joe transferred to Birmingham Southern College so he could live with his sister. He couldn't find a Free Will Baptist Church in the city, but there was a large Southern Baptist church about a mile from the college.

"I just knew I wasn't going to like West End Baptist," said Joe. "I thought all big city churches were cold, dead, worldly, and formal. I was wrong. The church was wonderful." Even though the young adults at the church had grown up together, they received Joe like he had always been a part of their group. He blossomed like a potted plant taken out of a dark corner and placed in the sunlight.

Joe rested his chin on his hand and looked thoughtful. "I knew I was called to ministry in April 1961. I was singing in the church choir on a Tuesday night. Suddenly, I felt a curtain had opened and I heard the Lord say, 'I want you in the ministry.' It wasn't an audible voice; it was much stronger than that."

Joe faced one of the greatest challenges in his ministry at a church in the Mississippi Delta. During the height of the civil rights movement, Joe preached God's love for all races. He was unaware of his congregation's struggle with his bold declaration until the chairman of the deacons approached him. "What you are preaching is correct," said the chairman, "but I want to remind you that the pastor who preceded you taught these people that segregation was God's way. You can change them, but you need to be patient."

Joe decided to place an advertisement in the local paper announcing "Visitors Sunday." His congregation was preparing packets to give visitors when they learned an integrated civil rights group planned to attend the church. "That would have been lovely for me," said Joe, "but some of the church members would have gone ballistic. The rumor mill went into overdrive, and I cried to the Lord for help."

God spared Joe the task of pacifying angry church members when the integrated group failed to appear, but the Lord honored his patience and prayers. A detective on the local police force shared Joe's burden for reaching young people with the gospel. They organized a Delta-wide crusade. Sixty churches participated in the December 1969 crusade held at a local high school. During the week, 3,500 young people filled the stadium with 5,000 in attendance on Sundays. The evangelist who spoke said it was the most integrated meeting he had ever attended.

Joe accepted a new pastorate at Columbus, Mississippi, in 1974. The people were more progressive than his last congregation. Several black students from Mississippi State University attended but had never joined the church. Even though the civil rights movement had calmed by the mid-70s, churches were still splitting over integration.

During a deacons meeting, one of the deacons asked the chairman, "What are we going to do if one of the blacks join the church?"

The wise chairman said, "Don't worry about it; Pastor has a plan."

Joe laughed. "My plan was to receive them, but I knew that's not what they had in mind."

The following year, Kezia Chogo approached Joe. "Dr. McKeever, I believe the Lord would have me join the church." Joe knew accepting Kezia as a member could tear his church apart, so he stalled for time. He assured Kezia it would be wonderful to have her as a member. He gave her a book on Baptist beliefs and instructed her to mark anything she had a question about. "Kezia already knew what Baptists believed," said Joe. "I needed time to enlist people to pray."

When Kezia finished reading the book, Joe spoke frankly and honestly. "Some of the members might object and say rude things when I present you for membership, but I have a plan." Since Kezia had been led to the Lord by Baptist missionaries, Joe was confident his missionary-minded church members would not reject the fruit of their labor. Kezia understood her pastor's predicament and agreed to give her testimony when he presented her for membership.

The rest of the week, Joe fasted, read his Bible, and prayed for God's intervention. One afternoon he read in Psalms, "They who fear the Lord will rejoice when they see you because you waited on the Lord." Joe paused and asked God what the verse meant. As he meditated, the meaning unfolded.

"'They who fear the Lord' are God's faithful people in the church," Joe explained. "'Will rejoice when they see you' meant the people would rejoice when I stood before them to recommend Kezia for membership. I knew this would happen because I waited on the Lord. I felt such a peace. I no longer needed to pray."

The following Sunday, Joe called Kezia to the front of the church and gave her the microphone. Kezia explained to the congregation how Baptist missionaries led her to the Lord. Four people voted against Kezia's membership. The rest of the church was thrilled and lined the walls to welcome Kezia as a member.

After the service, the congregation gathered around Joe and thanked him for removing the albatross of racism from around their necks. One of the men who voted against her said, "I wasn't against that girl, but I just felt like my old pappy wanted me to vote against her." The following semester, the man paid Kezia's college tuition.

I had listened to Joe's wit, wisdom, and humor for more than an hour and stood to leave. "Sit down," said Joe. "I want to sketch you." I left the café with my sketch and a truth I'll never forget. Sometimes God's people do bad things but their deeds are seldom malicious. Their actions can often be traced to bad doctrine that stunted their spiritual growth. If we are patient and wait on the Lord, righteousness will prevail.

A Ray of Hope

I opened an e-mail from a dear friend and read sad news: the economic troubles preceding the historic election of America's first black president had cost Milena Rimassa her job. I immediately sent her an e-mail expressing my concern. Her reply contained an air of confidence that all was well.

Several e-mails later, the dam broke and the truth flowed. Milena was in great distress. Her husband had lost his job several months before she did, and their savings had already been depleted by Hurricane Katrina. She didn't know how her family would survive.

I reminded Milena of the desire she had to minister to people struggling with addictions. "Perhaps God has shut a door so he could open another that would fulfill your desire." My words of hope were quenched by her pain. I prayed for my friend and gave her space and time to heal.

Three months later, I received an e-mail from Milena with the link to a website she thought would interest me. Her e-mail included a beautiful prayer. Clearly, God had healed her hurting heart. I gladly accepted her invitation to meet for coffee. She paid the bill—a sign she was no longer penniless. "I felt like I'd called God for help and he put me on hold for a long time, but he came through at the eleventh hour," said Milena.

"Did you feel a little like John the Baptist when he was in prison?" I asked.

"I felt more like the rat that was keeping John the Baptist company in prison." Milena laughed. "I never lost faith, but it was a struggle to keep up a façade for my daughter. She had already lost so much, first in hurricane Katrina, and then her father died a few months after the hurricane. I've been down several times in my life, but there is always a ray of hope."

Years earlier, a light dawned in Milena's heart after her mother died. Her mother had struggled with alcoholism and ended up in hospice by age fifty-nine. Milena visited her mother as often as possible. On one trip, her plane encountered turbulence and was forced to make an unscheduled landing. She called to tell her mother that she loved her and that she was on her way. Her mother had already died. "When I buried my mother, I realized that life is transitory and something bigger and grander is waiting," said Milena.

Milena returned to Los Angeles and a marriage already in jeopardy. Her husband's drug abuse had become intolerable. She had watched alcohol destroy her mother's life and decided she couldn't go through similar circumstances again. She begged her husband to get help. When he refused, she divorced him.

In need of a way to provide for her children, Milena started a business that became the precursor to Isis Films and worked as an executive selling global distribution rights for independent movies. She also produced several independent films: *Other Voices* (2000),

The Sterling Chase (1999), *Mel* (1998), *Waiting for the Rocket* (1994) and *For Parents Only* (1991).

"I believed in a higher power and lived accordingly, but I didn't call that power "God." That came after I married Trey. Life couldn't have been better. We both had executive jobs, nice cars, and we purchased a beautiful home," said Milena.

Trey was at work when Milena picked up her daughters, Lara and Nova. Lara called shotgun. She never let Lara ride in the front seat for safety reasons. They were only two miles from home, so Milena relented. They were almost home when a tow truck for eighteen-wheelers broadsided her car.

Milena's eyes filled with tears. "Thank God Lara called shotgun. If she had been sitting in the backseat and her sister had been sitting in the front, the crash would have killed Nova or anyone bigger than a child. The accident shattered the left side of my body. Somehow I found the strength to hold Lara in my arms and pray God would take me and let her live. We both lived, and it was in that moment that I knew God exists. My daughter survived the impossible."

The wreck had severed Milena's anterior cruciate ligament (ACL), one of the most important of four ligaments connecting the bones of the knee joint that provides stability by controlling backward and forward motion. Milena needed surgery to return to her normal activities, which included endurance walking.

Unable to work, her savings dwindled. Then Trey lost his job and the bank repossessed their home. Trey went to Baton Rouge to seek help from his mother and to look for employment. Milena remained in California to wait for a donor.

"If I couldn't walk, I couldn't work. I needed to work so I could care for my children. I began praying and attended church. It didn't matter to me which church. I just wanted God to put my life back in balance, heal my daughter, and let me walk again." The doctor was baffled when Milena's body developed scar tissue that acted like an ACL. He summoned his colleagues to examine her knee. They ordered X-rays and an MRI. Amazed by the unusual ACL, they repeatedly prodded and wiggled her knee to test its stability. After yet another MRI and another round of X-rays, the doctors concluded that she did not need surgery. Her knee was in better shape than it had been before the accident.

A few months later, Milena went hiking in the Grand Canyon with her favorite cousin. "Without the aid of a brace, Tanya and I walked nineteen continuous hours, only stopping to eat, air our feet, or rest briefly. The experience proved to me God had answered my prayer. When we reached the precipice, my feet were bleeding and blistered, but that didn't matter. I could walk."

Milena's voice broke with emotion. She wiped tears from her eyes as she continued her story. "I fell to my knees and prayed, 'From this point forward, I give my life to you. I don't need my free will. I need your will.' That happened the third weekend of September 2002, and I've never looked back."

I had joined Milena for coffee to learn how God turned her life around since our last e-mail. She gave me so much more, and then she told me how God came through at the eleventh hour. Her husband had obtained a job organizing events, and WLAE-TV hired Milena to produce the Prep Gridiron Report. Then God fulfilled her desire to help addicts. The Louisiana Department of Health and Human Resources asked Milena to produce Recovery Fest for the state's observance of the twentieth anniversary of National Recovery Month.

Milena produced an all-day event that included a benefit concert featuring music from Jefferson Starship, Big Brother and the Holding Company, Richie Havens, Cyril Neville, Lynyrd Skynyrd's Jo Jo Billingsly, and many more. The funds raised benefited rehabilitation facilities in the state of Louisiana, including Odyssey House, a behavioral health-care facility with an emphasis on addiction treatment; O'Brien House, a halfway house serving recovering alcoholics and drug addicts; Cenikor Foundation, specialist in helping people with chronic substance dependence; the Council on Alcoholism and Drug Abuse; and the Chemical Dependency Council.

Three months earlier, I had tried to comfort Milena by suggesting that God had shut a door so he could fulfill her desire. Clearly, God had directed my words. I wasn't a prophet predicting Milena's future, but I did offer a ray of hope that better things were on the horizon.

Trusting God

Robert Comeaux is the only one I did not have the pleasure of interviewing. I met Robert during a meeting with his church's pastor. At the time, I had an assistant the same age as Robert. I sent him to record Robert's story.

Robert's earliest memories of New Orleans are images of church classrooms filled with fidgeting children memorizing Bible verses. Of all the verses he memorized, he was drawn to Proverbs 3:5-6: "Trust in the Lord with all your heart and lean not on your own understanding; in all your ways acknowledge him, and he will make your paths straight."

The devoted Sunday school teachers never failed to invite their young students to talk about faith and about knowing Jesus in a personal way. At five years of age, Robert accepted the teacher's invitation and prayed for Jesus to forgive him for his sins and to lead him through life.

"Accepting Christ at such a young age sounds bizarre. How much could I have understood?" said Robert. "But Jesus talked about having faith like a child. Faith is cut-and-dried, simple. Even a five-year-old child can comprehend who Jesus is."

Robert's parents reinforced his salvation experience when they asked him if he understood the commitment he made. He assured his parents that he did. "That experience was a defining moment that convinced me God would guide my life," said Robert.

He entertained thoughts of entering the ministry but lacked clear direction as he walked onto the campus of Clifton Ganus, a small Christian high school. God used Carol, the school's choir director, and her husband, Jerry, to give Robert the direction he needed. After hearing Robert sing "Amazing Grace," Carol exclaimed, "God has given you a gift, and I'm going to help you develop that gift if I have to give you singing lessons for free." Jerry joined his wife's crusade and gave Robert piano lessons. When Robert's interest in music lapsed, Carol and Jerry gently prodded him back onto his God-ordained path.

Robert was admitted into the honors program at Palm Beach Atlantic University after graduating as the valedictorian of his class. He entered as a voice major but remained unsure about becoming a music minister. Traditional church music did not connect with Robert, who considered it a classical foundation for the contemporary styles he favored. He received the direction he needed during an internship at First Baptist West Palm Beach. By the time he finished the internship, he knew God had called him to music ministry.

After Robert's graduation, North Phoenix Baptist Church hired him to be its associate minister of music. He became a member of the Phoenix Chorale (formerly the Phoenix Bach Choir). In 2008, the Chorale's album, *Grechaninov: Passion Week*, was nominated for four Grammys. The album (a collaboration between the Phoenix Chorale and the Kansas City Chorale) won a Grammy for the "Best Engineered Album" in the classical category. The following year, the Phoenix Chorale won a Grammy for the "Best Small Ensemble Performance" in the classical category for its recording of "Spotless Rose: Hymns to the Virgin Mary," conducted by Charles Bruffy.

Robert's ministry and musical career were flourishing, but his destiny did not lie in Phoenix. The Sunday before Hurricane Katrina's landfall, Robert's heart was drawn to New Orleans as he watched reports about a massive storm in the Gulf of Mexico. Nine months later, Robert led a mission trip to New Orleans to gut houses. "While driving around the city, I said to one of the leaders, 'I can't imagine leaving North Phoenix, but if I did, I think God would call me to New Orleans. My heart is in this city.'"

More than a year later, Robert and his wife, Juliet, were praying for God's direction when a representative from First Baptist New Orleans called to tell him about the position of Associate Pastor of Worship and Music. The Comeauxs were offered the position, and they moved to New Orleans in November 2007. His office at the sprawling seventeen-acre campus of First Baptist gives him a view of downtown New Orleans, the city where he came to Christ with an unwavering childlike faith.

"I've always trusted God," said Robert. "I don't lean on my own understanding or trust too much in what I know. I have acknowledged him in all my ways, and he directed me back to the city closest to my heart."

The Bible concludes with the city closest to God's heart descending from heaven, prepared as a bride for her husband. Robert's experience gave me hope that God can bring us safely to the city he loves if we trust in the Lord and lean not on our own understanding.

He Brought Peace

At one time, Michelle Beadle, a Jewish believer in Jesus, and I attended the same congregation. Twice, I planned to attend the Passover Seder she hosted. Twice, circumstances beyond my control thwarted my plans. Then I left the congregation and lost touch with Michelle's ministry.

When a friend gave me a flyer announcing a Passover Seder sponsored by CJF Ministries at the Metairie Sheraton, I recognized the name of the New Orleans representative hosting the Seder: Michelle Beadle. I contacted Michelle and offered to write an article about the upcoming event. She accepted and consented to tell me her spiritual journey to faith in Jesus.

Michelle's journey began when her family survived the Holocaust. "Some people have the notion that you are only a Holocaust survivor if you survived the camps," said Michelle. "The true definition is someone who came out alive after the experience."

Aaron and Sarah, Michelle's grandparents on her mother's side of the family, applied for visas to come to America shortly after Hitler became Chancellor of Germany. At the time, immigration to America was limited by quotas. If the quota had been met, the immigrant needed a sponsor to deposit $1,500 in an American bank to guarantee the immigrant would never go on welfare.

Aaron and Sarah searched in vain for a sponsor as persecution increased. Jewish businesses were boycotted. Jews were denied health insurance. The Nuremberg Laws stripped them of citizenship and forbade them to marry non-Jews.

The Gestapo came to arrest Aaron twice. The first time, a member of the Stuttgart police warned Aaron that the Gestapo was coming but if he feigned sickness they would not arrest him. The second time, Aaron hid inside a neighbor's trunk for three days. The neighbor did not have room for Steven, Aaron's son, who fled, jumping from rooftop to rooftop until he reached a cousin's house. The cousin had already been arrested. Knowing the Gestapo would not return, he hid in the attic.

"My grandfather was a dermatologist in Germany," said Michelle. "One of his Gentile patients moved to America and found employment with a wealthy Jewish attorney in Manhattan. She convinced him to sponsor my mother, her parents, and brother."

By the time they obtained visas, Michelle's mother had been denied an education, and her grandfather could no longer practice medicine. Michelle's mother was thirteen when she boarded a train bound for Switzerland with her parents. Steven had already been sent to England.

When they arrived at the Swiss border, they were the only family ordered off the train. The German police rifled through their suitcases and even cut up a piece of sausage searching for hidden jewelry or money. The police waved them back on the train, and they traveled to England to pick up Steven.

Steven was supposed to stay with a family in the country, but the host family decided he was too much of a burden and didn't want him in their house. "My uncle Steven slept in a barn with animals for two years. When my mother and grandparents arrived, he didn't even have a coat to wear," said Michelle.

Aaron and Sarah rented a thirteen-bedroom apartment on the Upper Westside of Manhattan and opened a nursing home for elderly Jewish women. Sarah operated the nursing home to support the family. Aaron returned to medical school and obtained the necessary credentials to open a medical practice in America.

Michelle's family on her father's side lived a privileged life in Berlin. Her grandparents, Shlomo and Ruth, owned two homes staffed with maids, cooks, and a chauffeur. Shlomo worked as a manager of a business supply company until his boss reluctantly asked him to leave. Jewish men were no longer allowed to work in Germany. Shortly after Shlomo lost his job, the Gestapo came to arrest him. Ruth hid her husband in the attic and told the Gestapo that they had already arrested him. Her quick-witted action saved his life.

Shlomo and Ruth found a distant relative to sponsor them. They lost everything before they left Germany. "My grandfather Shlomo worked as a door-to-door peddler, and they lived the rest of their lives in poverty," said Michelle. "My father didn't have money to pay the toll for the subway, so he walked for miles to attend a vocational high school."

"Did the experience shake your parents' faith in God?" I asked Michelle.

"Christians have this idea that Jewish people automatically believe in God and have faith. Judaism is more than a faith. It's a culture, tradition, and a history. My family attended a synagogue in New York formed by German Jewish survivors of the Holocaust, but both my parents were agnostic. They never talked about God. None of my family did," said Michelle.

As a child, Michelle was captivated by a statue of Jesus in a Catholic cemetery that her family drove past on their way to synagogue. "I was strangely attracted to it. Every time we went to synagogue, I couldn't wait to see it. No one told me it was a statue of Jesus. I knew it was, and I thought it was beautiful."

After high school, Michelle was accepted at Cornell University. "My lifelong dream to attend Cornell was fulfilled, and I didn't have any more goals to achieve," said Michelle. "In my senior year, I became anxious about my future."

Michelle searched for purpose and meaning by reading everything she could find on spirituality. She dismissed most of what she read as impractical until a friend gave her *The Late Great Planet Earth* by Hal Lindsay. Lindsay's book explained God's plan and purpose for Israel. She found his arguments that Jesus fulfilled the prophecies about the Messiah were convincing.

"When I finished the book, I prayed for the first time in my life. 'God, I know you know all things.'" Michelle laughed. "Up to this point in my life, I never thought about God, yet all of a sudden I knew God knew all things. I prayed, 'I don't know if I should believe what I've read. You've got to show me the truth.' Somehow I was able to trust God would do that even though I had never trusted God for anything in the past."

Within three months, Michelle encountered three Christians. First, she met Malaer at the university library. They quickly developed a close friendship. "What I experienced with Malaer was unconditional love. I'd always dreamed of having a friend who was like a sister because I only had a brother. Malaer became that friend," said Michelle.

Then a date brought Michelle to a fraternity party where a member of Campus Crusade for Christ shared his faith with them. Michelle felt embarrassed by his intrusion, but she wanted to hear what he was saying.

Later, Michelle noticed a woman in her nutrition class who was full of joy and wondered how someone could be so happy. As they walked to the dorm, Michelle asked her why she was so happy. The woman responded, "I believe in Jesus." Enraged by her answer, Michelle belittled her for believing a man could heal people.

In December of that year, Malaer and Michelle attended a conference for social workers. During lunch, a stranger sat at their table and shared her faith in Jesus with Michelle. As the woman told her story, Michelle saw Malaer nodding in agreement and felt betrayed.

"Before I could lambaste her like I did the other woman," said Michelle, "I felt something inside me say 'Listen to Malaer. She loves you.'" Michelle asked Malaer why she agreed with the stranger. Malaer explained that she was raised in a Hindu family in Malaysia but an aunt who had embraced Jesus as the one true God led her to salvation.

"I believe God sent Malaer halfway around the world to tell this Jewish girl from New York City about the Messiah. I wouldn't have received the message from anyone else. Being a first-generation American child of Holocaust survivors, I felt more comfortable with European culture than American culture. Malaer was from a different culture, and I was very comfortable with her. Before lunch ended, I prayed with Malaer, asking Jesus to come into my heart. Instantly, all of the anxiety I had been wrestling with left. I felt at peace with myself and with God. Jewish people say Jesus cannot be the Messiah because he did not bring political peace to Earth. He may not have brought political peace, but he brought spiritual peace between God and Man."

I love the Jewish people. Michelle helped me understand Jewish culture, and I'll never forget how another Jewish friend defended me. Otto had recently joined the secular writers critique group I attended. The unbelievers in the group usually struggled to maintain a civil composure when they commented on my material. That night their comments were more contentious than usual. I bit my tongue as some of the writers expressed harsh opinions about me and Jesus.

Otto commented last. "I'm a Jew, and I don't believe in Jesus, but this is damn fine material." I picked my jaw up off the floor and refrained from laughing as Otto chastised the group for thinking my material was anything less. My Jewish Savior brought peace to the writers group through a Jew who didn't even believe in him. In Michelle's words, Messiah Jesus, "shall be called Pele-joez-el-gibbor-Avi-AD-sar-shalom: wonderful counselor (Pele-joez); the mighty God (el-gibbor); the everlasting father (Avi-AD); the prince of peace (sar-shalom).

Engulfed in Fire

The pastor of Iglesia VIDA church had recently made application to join the Assemblies of God Fellowship. I had been asked to write Pastor Wade Moody's profile for the New Orleans Section website, so my husband and I visited his church. I was impressed to see the children given an active part in the service. A young girl prayed, I think; it was a Spanish service. A young boy received the offering. Several children danced before the Lord and waved colorful flags. It was difficult to be still as I filmed the worship. I wanted to put my camera down and dance with them.

Dalyz, one of the congregation members, translated the pastor's message for us. Pastor Wade told me it would be a summary. I think Dalyz gave us more than a summary. We were invited to stay for a meal after the service, but God had blessed the afternoon garage sale and all the food had been sold. I'm thinking that was a good thing since they were in the process of purchasing the gym that serves as their church.

After the service I sat with Pastor Moody in a room that had been converted into an office. His soft-spoken manner contrasted his passionate zeal for Christ. I turned on my recorder. The story that followed left me in awe of God's love and protection.

Wade Mateo Moody was born into a good family. His parents ran a successful business, which employed much of their extended family. Wade and his siblings were well behaved and excelled in school. Neither drug nor alcohol abuse found access into their tight-knit clan.

Wade was six years old when his parents questioned the validity of Christianity and embarked on a quest to find the truth. For the next nine years, he experienced a host of philosophies and Asian religions. The discontent in his parents' lives created a cancer that destroyed the foundation of Wade's happy home. His parents divorced when he was fifteen. Everyone went his or her own way, leaving Wade to fend for himself on the streets of Honduras.

"By the time I was seventeen, I gave up on God," said Wade. "What was the point of being 'good' when my family lived a good life and it didn't keep us from being torn apart? I decided my parents never should have married and I never should have been born. If there was a God, I was too insignificant for him to care about."

Wade moved to Tegucigalpa, the capital of Honduras, to open a computer school. Lacking equipment and financial backing, the business failed, but he made close friends during the venture. When local gangs harassed his friends, they realized the necessity of helping one another.

"We didn't intend to start a new gang, but that is what we became," said Wade. "We were different. We had drugs and street fighting, but we also had brains. We designed our gang to protect ourselves from other gangs and from the police."

The city of Tegucigalpa had a zero-tolerance policy for gangs. The police beat gang members without reprisal. Sometimes gangs disappeared without explanation. Wade and his friends took advantage of government connections and applied for credentials as GEDE, a group organized to assist in disasters and emergencies. The credentials gave them access to military training and permission to carry weapons.

"At the time, there were a lot of mudslides causing disasters. The government would call us to assist in rescue operations, but it was just a cover. Privately, we joked, 'We are specialist in disasters; we make the disasters.' The credentials gave us privileges other gangs didn't have. If we fought a rival gang and the police showed up, we showed them our credentials. They let us go and arrested the other gang. That made us a popular gang to join. Ironically, the gang we formed for protection carried a high price. Our popularity made us a target of the other gangs. I couldn't leave home without arming myself."

Wade's mother returned to Honduras when he was nineteen and settled on Isla del Tigre (Tiger Island), also known as Amapala. Her neighbors gave her gospel tracts and asked her if she had ever been born again. She was reluctant to receive their message but consented to read the Bible they gave her. As she read the scriptures, she found the truth that religious indoctrination had failed to impart. Jesus is humanity's Savior. He alone is the way to God. She prayed with her neighbors to be "born again." Shortly thereafter, she began attending Brigades of Christian Love, a Pentecostal church founded by Swiss missionaries.

"My mom sent me letters about being 'born again' and speaking in tongues. We had been through so many other spiritual things, I wrote it off as another religious fad. One day, I received a Bible in the mail. She had highlighted everything Jesus said in red. The enclosed letter said, "Please read the Gospel of John." Reading the Gospel was like reading a history book. It meant nothing to me."

As the economy in Honduras worsened, Wade's mother seized the opportunity to separate Wade from his gang. "Go to the states and live with your brother, she said. "You can get a job there and return to school." Wade knew his mother was right. His business ventures had failed, and it was increasingly difficult to cover expenses with his low-paying job.

"I figured if I went to the states and worked for a while, I could save money to buy computers. When I returned, I could reopen the computer school, and my gang would be the biggest, baddest gang in town. In addition to the other benefits our gang offered, we would own a business. I made arrangements to live with my brother in New Orleans."

GEDE arranged a party to show their support of Wade's new venture. A week before the party, his mother called. "Wade, you will be leaving for the states soon, and I don't know when you will be back. I'd like to spend time with you before you go. My church is going to a youth camp near Tegucigalpa. Why don't you come for a few days? There are more than four hundred young people attending."

The large number of young people captured Wade's interest. He held the position of recruiter in GEDE. His labors had increased the gang from the original seven to a hundred. He wanted to spend time with his mother, but he also saw a field ripe for harvesting new recruits into his gang.

Early Monday morning, Wade drove his motorcycle onto the campgrounds and saw a former gang member. He followed him, thinking the man would help recruit others. Wade was confused to learn the man had converted to Christianity and wasn't interested in rejoining the gang.

Wade spent the rest of the day evangelizing for the dark side to no avail. He walked into the evening service frustrated over his failure to recruit anyone and sat next to his mother. The congregation began singing songs about fire coming from heaven and praying God would send his fire to burn in them. Wade associated fire with hell. He shifted uncomfortably in his seat, looked for the exit, and then looked at his mother.

"What kind of church is this? I don't want to be in the fire."

She assured him they were only singing about the Holy Spirit and his power.

After the service, a young man escorted Wade to a cot in one of the cabins. He lay down for a fitful night's sleep. The morning light that shone through the cabin window could not dispel the dark depression clouding Wade's mind. By late afternoon, he abandoned his evangelistic plans and walked up a nearby hill and sat on a log. His position on the hill gave him a view of most of the campground. His eyes traveled from a group playing basketball to another group sitting in a circle talking and laughing. Other groups were praying, and some strummed guitars, singing praises to God.

Envy flashed in Wade's heart. "I think I converted sitting on that log, because I realized they had what I had been looking for. I tried to fill the emptiness in my life with everything I could think of and surrounded myself with a gang for safety. At the end of the day, I was just a scared kid living in fear that any minute someone would crash through the door and kill me. God seldom speaks to our ears. He speaks directly to our heart, and I heard his voice clearly that day. The Christians had something better than I had, and I wanted to join their gang."

Wade knew he had to attend the party GEDE had planned for him the following night. He wasn't leaving until he walked down the dirt floor to the altar in the roughly constructed shack without windows or air conditioning that served as a church. He found a seat near one of the two lightbulbs illuminating the building.

"Turn to John 14:6," said the preacher.

Wade opened the Bible his mother had given to him and read, "I am the way the truth and the life. No one comes to the father except through me." Another light flipped on dispelling the darkness, not in the dimly lit church, but the darkness in Wade's mind. At the conclusion of the message, he ran to the altar and prayed Jesus would accept him into the Christian gang. He could hear his mother shouting and screaming for joy in the background.

That night, Wade lay on his cot, quietly forgiving those who had hurt him. "As I forgave my mom, my dad, and anyone else I could think of, I felt engulfed in fire from my head to my toe. It felt like lava was flowing through my veins. The next day, my mother told me it was the Holy Spirit. In retrospect, if I had not had that experience, I don't think I could have done what I did at the party."

Wade returned to Tegucigalpa and walked into the hall that had been rented for his party. As he milled through the eighty-five members that were present, he heard, "What happened to you?"

He turned to see who was talking.

"You look different," someone else said.

Wade didn't understand what they meant.

"Your face, there is something different about your face."

Then Wade realized they were seeing the new person he had become, and he was a lamb among wolves.

The president of the gang silenced the room and said to Wade, "Tonight is your night. Anything you want is yours. You say it. We do it."

"I want to form a circle," said Wade.

The crowd quickly formed a jagged circle and joined hands. "Are we going to fight each other?"

"No. As my last official act before I leave, I want us to pray."

The music stopped. Jaws dropped. Foreheads furrowed, wondering if their ears had betrayed them. Some stared as though an alien had invaded their midst.

Wade swallowed; his mouth dry. He suddenly realized he didn't know how to pray but had to finish what he started. "Yesterday I accepted Jesus as my Savior, and I want to pray for you. Jesus, please do for them what you did for me. Amen."

Wade walked through the stunned crowd and out the door. He mounted his motorcycle and drove a few blocks up a hill, where he stopped to see what would happen next. Leaving the gang was like leaving the Mafia. It's not done without consequences. He watched the lights in the hall flip off one by one as gang members exited and drove away.

Fear gripped Wade. He drove around the city, wondering when they would catch him. He finally pulled in front of his apartment. The lights were on, and the vehicles of the gang's leaders were parked nearby. Wade parked his bike and resigned himself to his fate.

As soon as Wade stepped into his apartment, one of the leaders said, "Are you really a Christian? Did you really do that?" The agitation in his voice increased Wade's fear.

"Yes," said Wade. "I love you guys, but I can't live like this anymore."

Two of the leaders leaped to their feet, muttering curses as they stormed out of the tiny apartment. Four remained. Wade braced himself for the beating that was sure to follow.

One of the leaders said, "We want to know Jesus too. We don't know what happened to you, but we want what you have."

Wade sighed with relief. "You just need to tell Jesus you want him in your life."

Wade and his friends talked late into the night. Before they left, he promised to bring them to church on Sunday.

Wade's thoughts returned to the camp. Returning on a motorcycle without headlights would be dangerous. Thoughts about the camp persisted, so he locked his apartment door and made the two-hour drive to the youth camp. At 4 a.m., he knocked on the cabin door, where he had laid on his cot the previous night engulfed in the fire of God.

"Who is it?" a timid voice whispered.

"It's Wade."

"Wade? Wade!" An echo of "Wade is back" reverberated throughout the cabin as sleepy campers realized their prayer had been answered.

Wade stood at the locked door listening to the joy erupting within. He pounded on the door again. "Guys, let me in."

When someone realized the object of their joy was standing outside, he unlocked the door. Wade walked into a flood of love. They hugged him repeatedly and wept. "We've been praying for you to come back."

Wade remained at the camp the rest of the week and then returned home to keep his promise. Sunday morning, the gang leaders arrived with fifteen gang members. All of them wanted to attend church.

"When we walked into the church," said Wade, "the people parted like the Red Sea. I thought they were being nice and giving us their seats." Wade smiled. "They were afraid of us. At the end of the sermon, every gang member went to the altar to receive Christ. I've kept in touch with them through the years. All of them are still committed Christians. Most became pastors."

A Spiritual Gift

The first time I met Pastor Anthony Freeman, he had just placed a bid on a Methodist church damaged by Hurricane Katrina. I wrote an article about his efforts to plant a church in Uptown New Orleans. After he won the bid, he took me on a tour of the building and then sat on one of the mahogany pews donated to the church to tell me his story.

When Anthony was seven years old, he watched a Billy Graham crusade on TV and prayed for salvation. His heart strayed from God when he entered his teenage years, but he did not have the option of abandoning church. His devout Christian parents never missed a service.

His mother sensed something was wrong in her son's life. Her fear was confirmed when she discovered his plan to skip church and spend the evening with a girl. She confronted Anthony with a stern rebuke. "My mother's rebuke convicted me of my sin. I went into the bathroom to cry and recommitted my life to Christ."

Several months later, Anthony met a man who guided him through a one-month discipleship school. The strict boot camp-style program demanded exercise, work, Bible study, and evangelism. They met early in the morning to jog and then read ten chapters of the Bible. Bible studies were held morning and afternoon with manual labor in between. After dinner, they walked the streets sharing Christ and participated in community outreaches on the weekends.

"That experience solidified my Christianity and shaped me into an evangelist, but I didn't have thoughts of being a minister. I planned to be a doctor," said Anthony. "I was praying when God spoke to me in a voice that permeated my entire being calling me to ministry. My father questioned my decision to attend Bible college instead of medical school, but my mother knew I was predestined for ministry."

During his first week at college, Anthony's love for evangelism stirred him to join a group of students who ministered at a nearby park. Melanie, a beautiful woman from Canada, caught his eye. He hoped she would be his ministry partner. She later confessed to the same desire. Several years later, Anthony proposed, and they became partners for life.

The Freemans were pastors when they met three ministers with a common dream: a Bible college that offered an affordable education to young ministers. Through much prayer and hard work, their dream became a reality. The New Orleans School of Urban Missions (SUM) opened in 1992, and then they launched a second campus in Oakland, California, in 1999. Anthony served SUM for thirteen years, first as a professor and then as president. His final two years at SUM, he presided over both campuses, flying from New Orleans to Oakland and back every two weeks.

Anthony thought he had found his final destination in ministry, but God had other plans. By August 2004, Anthony knew he would resign as the school's president. A year later, he submitted his resignation while at the Oakland campus. On the flight back to New Orleans, Anthony pondered the decade of service he had given to the students of SUM, and sadness swept over him.

In an attempt to relieve his depression, he joined his four sons in a game of basketball. During the game, Anthony severely broke his ankle. The doctor immediately put his foot in a cast, which restricted the swelling. The unbearable pain distracted Anthony from the foreboding newscasts of a monster storm heading toward New Orleans. By the end of the week, a flurry of activity to secure SUM and send the students to the safety of the Oakland campus left little time to indulge his depression. He left the city with his family as the feeder bands of Katrina came ashore.

FEMA's slow response to the disaster forced the mayor of Gretna, a community adjoining New Orleans, to seek help from other venues. The mayor knew SUM had contacts with organizations that could supply food and water. Two days after the storm, he sent Anthony a letter that gave him access through government checkpoints into the city.

Anthony returned to a city in chaos. "When we entered Gretna, it looked like a bomb had exploded," said Anthony. He found the mayor in the public utilities building trying to save their city as water pumps continued to fail. He followed the mayor to his office in City Hall. As they entered the building, a group of police officers rushed out the door to help firemen who were dodging bullets as they attempted to quench the fire set by looters at Oakwood Mall.

The weary and discouraged mayor gladly allowed Anthony to pray for him. SUM became the hub for faith-based groups that came to rebuild the city. Every morning, Anthony met with the mayor and then dispatched volunteers to the areas of greatest need.

As Anthony's official last day with SUM approached, the Freemans decided to visit Melanie's family in Canada while they pondered what to do next. They were on the highway between Ontario and Toronto discussing offers from various churches when they heard the Lord say, "Return to New Orleans and start a church."

The Freemans were undaunted by the lack of a church building. "We decided that you don't have to be in a church building to worship God," said Anthony, "so we started the church in my living room." They offered a home-cooked meal and Bible study to the volunteers surviving on army-issued MREs (meals ready to eat). Volunteers from Pennsylvania, Kansas, Texas, and California accepted their invitation and became the core team that launched All Nations Fellowship.

All Nations Fellowship held its first service on Easter Sunday, April 2007. The congregation consisted of the core team, a few families, and some homeless people until Tofu walked into the church. Tofu's story began when Anthony was president of SUM. Anthony helped Tesia, his administrative assistant and spiritual daughter, raise funds to return to Mozambique and work with Iris Ministries. The ministry was baptizing converts when Tofu, a young medical student from Boston, stopped to photograph the event and witnessed people receive the gift of tongues. When Tesia learned Tofu was on his way to New Orleans to attend Tulane University, she encouraged him to visit Anthony's church.

Tofu, an Episcopalian, knew nothing about the gift of tongues except what he had witnessed in Africa. When he visited All Nations Fellowship, he questioned Anthony about the experience and expressed a desire to receive the gift. "I prayed God would give him the gift, and he spoke in tongues for three hours. I got tired of praying with him and left," said Anthony. "Tofu was a blessing. He brought a lot of students to the church, increasing our membership."

The gift of speaking in other tongues surfaced more than once as I've talked to people from various denominations. A Lutheran informed me people don't speak in tongues anymore. That has not been my experience. Some privately confessed to me that they possess the gift of tongues but are reluctant to create problems within their church. A Baptist told me, "I don't speak with tongues, but who am I to say what God will and won't give us? If he did it once, he could do it again." The Bible agrees. "Every good and perfect gift is from above, coming down from the Father of the heavenly lights, who does not change like shifting shadows" (James 1:17).

Prodigal Daughter

I thoroughly enjoyed Christa Allan's funny, refreshingly honest presentation at the Southern Christian Writer's Guild and invited her to meet with me. As we sipped coffee at PJ's Coffee House, she gave me more than I expected. Her poignant story of faith lost, faith found, and faith shared dropped from her lips like puzzle pieces waiting for assimilation.

Spurned by the high school "in" crowd, Christa learned that she could escape the harsh realities of life with words. She wrote imaginative stories that vilified her abusers. When a friend complimented one of her stories, Christa sought a second opinion from her teacher. The teacher's encouraging comments convinced Christa that she had a talent for writing.

"My first husband liked to say, 'Those who can, do, those who can't, teach'," said Christa. "I taught English, so I didn't pursue being published."

Her life fell apart when her daughter was born with Down syndrome. She turned to the church for an explanation. "Why can God raise Lazarus from the dead but he can't fix my child?" Christa demanded.

The priest studied his distraught parishioner. "You may not want to hear this right now, but I want you to think about this: Lazarus died twice." His response failed to dispel Christa's frustration with the Almighty, so she abandoned the church and consoled herself with alcohol.

"A friend got in my face and told me, 'You drink too much,'" said Christa. "She refused to give up on me until I agreed to talk to a counselor at a rehabilitation hospital. The counselor convinced me I had a problem."

Christa entered an in-house rehab program. Thirty days later, she walked out of the hospital with instructions to visit Alcoholics Anonymous, a support group that helps members maintain sobriety through dependence on a higher power. "Alcoholics Anonymous brought me back to God," said Christa. "I knew I couldn't do this alone, and to me the higher power was God." Christa returned to faith in God, but she didn't return to the church."

The following year, her marriage ended in divorce. Her now ex-husband agreed to keep their children until she adjusted to her new life. Christa's new life included Ken, a Jewish veterinarian. Shortly after Christa married Ken, a friend invited her to church. She enjoyed the service but wasn't prepared for the unexpected follow-up visit. She had been married less than a month when her Jewish husband returned home to find three Christian men in suits sitting in his den. She never returned to the church.

Christa prayed for a way to provide a spiritual foundation for her children when they came to live with her. A friend encouraged her to invest in her emotional commitment to God with a financial commitment. She chose a church down the street from her home and began mailing small donations from her salary.

A month later, Christa received a call from the recipient of her donations. A woman said, "Is this Christa Allan?"

"Yes."

"I'm the secretary at the First Baptist Church. Our pastor would like to speak to you." While Christa waited, she wondered what she had done to warrant a call from the pastor.

"Hello, this is Pastor Bailey. I was wondering why you started sending money to our church. We checked the roles. You're not a member."

"I know," said Christa. "We just moved here, and a friend told me I should invest in my emotional commitment to God with a financial one. Your church is near my house, so it made sense to send you some money."

"Okay, you probably don't know that most churches don't get money on a regular basis from people they don't know."

"I never thought about that," said Christa.

Christa met with Pastor Bailey shortly after he called. She was very comfortable with the personable pastor. "I liked that his wife taught in the public schools and his daughters attended a public high school. It spoke volumes about his faith and commitment to the community. I felt that I could connect with this church. Ken didn't mind as long as I didn't bother him with it. He just didn't get this Jesus thing, so I didn't force my faith on him."

Christa joined the church and increased her giving from small donations to a tithe. Shortly, after she increased her contributions, Ken told her that he needed to talk to her. She braced for a disagreement about money. Instead, Ken announced, "I'm going to talk to your pastor." Several months later, Ken accepted Christ and was baptized in the church. "My pastor calls him a completed Jew, and I really like that," said Christa.

Ken encouraged Christa to pursue publishing her writing. She was reluctant until she discovered Kristin Billerbeck's Christian fiction. "I wrote two one-page stories and e-mailed them to Kristin. I don't know what I was thinking and didn't expect her to respond, but she did. She said the stories had a great beginning but needed some structure. Her encouragement and my husband's support were all I needed," said Christa.

One day Christa was flipping through her journal and stopped to read an entry. She decided that she could do something with those thoughts and began writing her debut novel. When her enthusiasm for the project waned, Ken bought her a laptop. His gift spurred her to continue writing.

When friends in Christian publishing said a story about alcoholism would never sell, she abandoned the novel to write about safer themes. "I studied the market for articles that were selling and tried to write about the same things, but it was like putting an octopus in a box. I finally decided to write my book whether it sells or not."

Christa's manuscript eventually found its way into the hands of a literary agent who loved the story. God fulfilled Christa's lifelong dream of being a published author when Abingdon Press released her debut novel, *Walking on Broken Glass*.

The Bible tells us to "...encourage one another and build each other up..." (1 Thessalonians 5:11). Christa's story is a good example of why we should do so. Words of discouragement suppressed her gift for writing. Words of encouragement drew out her God-given talent to deal with, in Christa's words, "the elephant in the room." *Walking on Broken Glass* addressed Christians caught in alcoholism. The following year, *Edge of Grace* dealt with homosexual Christians. Her latest offering, *Love Finds You in New Orleans*, addresses mixed race relationships.

A Lot from a Little

Sonya McLean, Director of Women's Ministry Unlimited, invited me to write about her fall conference speaker, Cissy Padgett, missionary and recording artist. Cissy welcomed me into her hotel room and taught me a new word derived from music and missionary. "My husband and I are "musicianaries"—musical missionaries—but he doesn't travel with me often. He has to work to support my habit." Cissy laughed. "Ministry," she explained. "Few people will take a gospel tract from me, but rarely does someone turn down a free CD."

Cissy's father served as an Assembly of God pastor until marital infidelity destroyed his ministry and marriage. When Cissy was eleven years old, her mother packed their belongings. They went to Florida and never returned.

"I walked away from my faith when I entered high school, but Mother didn't give us an option about attending church. I made her life a misery," said Cissy. "Through all the trouble my mother endured, she retained her faith in God. I heard more than one person say, 'Betty, how can you hang on to the Lord? You were married to a minister, and now you are raising your girls alone.' I'll never forget my mother's answer: 'God is all I have to hold on to.'"

After Cissy married her high school sweetheart, she wanted to return to church, but her husband wasn't interested. Bill was raised as a Baptist, so Cissy joined a

Southern Baptist church, hoping he would follow. He didn't, but he never prevented Cissy from attending.

"The Baptist church was wonderful. I actively participated in its ministries, but my heart wasn't right with God. My attempt to fill a void with religious activities didn't work. I went to the altar so often one of the altar workers told me I must be saved or I wouldn't be so concerned about my salvation. I was looking for a feeling, an emotion, something I could point to as evidence of my salvation."

One night, Cissy dreamed Jesus had come to catch his church away to heaven, and she was left behind. She attempted to follow, using her arms as wings, but tired easily and kept falling to the earth. Finally, she fell from the sky into a standing dead tree. "I've got you now." The devil laughed and pulled her out of the tree.

Terrified, Cissy awoke, and a line from an old hymn came to mind: "There's room at the cross for you. Though millions have come, there's still room for one. There's room at the cross for you."

"That is when I knew that the Lord was still calling me and there was still hope for me," said Cissy.

Cissy and her sister, Brenda, were returning from a trip to St. Petersburg when her heart pounded with anxiety. "I knew the Lord was pursuing me, and I was tired. I couldn't run anymore." Cissy confessed her spiritual struggle to Brenda and asked to talk to Brenda's pastor.

Pastor Vester Raburn had known Cissy's family for many years. He listened patiently and then put his arm around her, and they knelt in front of his couch to pray.

"I didn't feel better after we prayed, but I just knew if I went to Pastor Raburn's church on Wednesday night, I would meet God."

Cissy walked into the church and met her grandmother at the altar. Grandma read scriptures to Cissy, assured her Jesus loved her, and prayed Cissy would release her fears. "After Grandma prayed with me, I felt the floodgates of heaven opening up, yet I still didn't sense the freedom I longed for. My mother, grandmother, and great-grandmother embraced faith, making it natural to love the Lord, but for me, accepting his forgiveness was a process.

Cissy returned to the Assembly of God church she had abandoned and began singing gospel music with her sisters. Their trio quickly grew to twenty-two members, including a live band. They traveled from church to church spreading the gospel through music. "My husband often traveled with us, loading and unloading the van. I remember seeing him sitting in the services clutching the pew in front of him so hard it would shake as he struggled with conviction."

One night, Cissy and Bill were sitting in church when their youngest daughter began to cry. Cissy took her to the nursery. A woman in the nursery shared how her husband had walked away from God. She didn't believe he would ever come back. Cissy felt the Lord quicken her heart. "I will never say that. My husband may not get saved tonight, or next week, but I know he will come to know Jesus as his Savior." Cissy picked up her daughter and returned to the service. Bill squeezed Cissy's hand when the minister called people to the altar. Thinking he wanted to leave, she picked up her baby and summoned her daughters. Bill motioned for them to sit down and stepped into the aisle. Instead of leaving, he went to the altar.

"My husband was a tough ol' dude, but God changed that. Today he is a church board member and can't talk about the Lord without crying."

One summer, Cissy's family vacationed at a campground in North Carolina. People at the campground said, "If you think this is great, you should see Glacier National Park in Montana."

The following year they visited Glacier National Park. "When we got to Montana, there was something that said 'home.' We returned several years in a row, and one day I said to my husband, 'Why don't we live where we love and vacation to see our family?' Bill was a native born Floridian. He wasn't interested in moving to Montana."

Several years later, Cissy attended a Teen Challenge meeting. A woman said she was terrified God would call her as a missionary to Africa. Cissy sprang to her feet and said, "God will never call you anywhere he has not first placed the desire to go." In that moment, Cissy realized God had given her the desire to move to Montana.

"I truly believe God fulfills the desires of your heart because he gave you the desire. I thought my desire to move to Montana was selfish. It never occurred to me the desire came from God."

God brought Bill into agreement with Cissy's desire at a most inopportune time. Bill announced he had resigned his job after their eldest daughter announced her engagement, and Cissy couldn't drive due to a recent surgery. Undeterred, they loaded up the kids, the newlyweds, and the dog and headed west. The house they rented had been sold when they arrived. A one-room cabin with a five-gallon hot water tank became their home for the next seven weeks.

They settled on attending Helena First Assembly of God, where a five-dollar challenge launched Cissy into her musical missionary work. Her pastor and mentor, Ken Ross, gave everyone in the congregation $5. He instructed them to invest the money for the kingdom of God and he would collect the earnings in sixty days.

Cissy loved the idea. Her sisters were scheduled to visit, so she used her five dollars to make posters announcing a gospel music concert. The offering received at the end of the concert multiplied her five-dollar investment into $1,400. Invitations to sing poured in, and Cissy continued giving 100 percent of profits from the concerts to missions.

"One day Pastor Ken told me I needed to make a CD. I left his office thinking he was nuts, but he kept watering that seed until it took root. I really liked music produced by The Ruppes, a gospel group formed by Leo and Brenda Ruppe and their daughters, so I contacted them to request their music. Leo answered the phone. When he learned I wanted to make a CD to support missions, he offered to help. He found a producer and studio I could use, but I needed to raise $10,000 within six weeks. I don't even remember how the money was raised. God blessed me, and when the deadline arrived, I had the money."

Pastor Ken's five-dollar-challenge did much more than raise money for missionary work—he launched a ministry. Cissy speaks at women's conferences across the country. She recorded her first CD, *He's Everything*, in 2004. Since the release of her debut CD, she has traveled to five countries, sharing the gospel through song, and recorded five more CDs: *Wonder* (2005), *Sweeter As the Days Go By* (2007), *Broken and Restored* (2009), *By the Way of the Cross* (2010), *Just Can't Keep From Singing* (2011). She also wrote two children's books, *Singing with Noah* and *First King of Rock*. A lot can come from a little.

Teena Myers

It's Not What You Can Do

Hearing the gospel preached and taught at Sunday school, church services, and fiery revivals filled George Zanca's childhood. The first sermon he preached predated his salvation. At the tender age of eight, he heard some of the older boys say God had called them to ministry. He blurted out, "God has called me to ministry too." George's mother heard her son's declaration and brought it to the attention of the pastor.

"George," said the pastor, "I hear you are called to ministry."

George hesitated. He planned to say, "No," but, "Yeah, I believe I am," came out of his mouth.

"Good, next week you are preaching the sermon."

George went home terrified and told his mother he was not going to church next Sunday. His wise, godly mother gave him a pamphlet about a little lost sheep named Wuggins that explained the salvation story.

"Read this pamphlet next Sunday. That will be all the preaching you have to do," she said.

"I read the pamphlet and ran back to my seat," said George. "At the time I made that statement, I never dreamed it was true or that God would hold me accountable for what I said."

Two years later, the heavy presence of God filled a church service. Intrigued by the people praising God and speaking in different languages, ten-year-old George walked to the altar to see what was happening. His mother joined him and led him in a prayer of repentance.

"You need to receive the Holy Spirit too," she said.

Obeying his mother's counsel, George prayed, "Lord, fill me with your Spirit." Suddenly, he was speaking in a different language.

The pursuit of girls replaced his commitment to Christ by the time he was fifteen. His parents forced him to attend church. The presence of his girlfriend, Jody, made the services tolerable, but he wasn't interested in God.

Stifled by the resistance George and Jody's parents had to their children's relationship, George asked Jody to elope. She agreed, left a note for her parents, and traveled to Kilgore, Texas, where they married. George savored the taste of freedom and vowed to be his own man. No one would tell him what he could do again, including his new wife. When they returned to New Orleans, Jody attended an Assembly of God church with George's mother. Pastor David Savage led her to accept Christ as her Savior. For the next five difficult years of her marriage, Jody prayed George would return to his faith.

"In December of 1976, George went to Texas with his brother and a friend," said Jody. "I knew they were up to no good, and I was worried. I was at a prayer meeting interceding for George when a woman came to pray with me and spoke a word of knowledge: 'Jesus says don't worry about your husband. I have him in my hand. He has a call on his life. He will return to me, and you will have a son.' Within a year, George returned to church, and I gave birth to our son."

George picked up the story. "Toward the end of 1976 a coworker tried to share his faith with me. I knew enough from attending church as a child that he was wrong, and I searched the Bible for scriptures to prove it. The debate continued for months. Then we got into a discussion about who was going to heaven. I looked for scriptures that proved I was going to heaven, and he wasn't. I could not find anything to prove my point. You could say God spoke to me. I had this feeling in my heart and mind that I could not find anything because I wasn't going to heaven. For the first time, I realized that studying to prove someone wrong had only proved that I was wrong."

January 12, 1977, George walked into his bedroom, where Jody was dressing for church and changed clothes.

Thinking George was going out with his friends, as he often did when she was at church, Jody asked, "Where are you going?"

His answer surprised her. "I'm going to church with you."

"I can't tell you what Pastor Savage preached that night," said George. "I was waiting for the altar call so I could repent, but he didn't give one. I felt like God was saying, 'If you really want to repent, you will come on your own.' When the service concluded, Pastor Savage said the altars were open if anyone wanted to pray. I ran to the altar and told Pastor Savage, 'I don't know where heaven is, but I want to go there.'"

George became a willing servant of God. He cleaned the church, changed diapers in the nursery, taught Sunday School, served as director of Sunday school, and led Royal Rangers, Men's Ministry, and Altar Workers Ministry. He also sang with the worship team and served as a deacon and an interim pastor. The only ministry he didn't experience was Women's Ministry. Over the years, numerous people asked why he wasn't pastoring a church. He always responded, "That is not what God called me to do."

He didn't think he was qualified to be a pastor. For many years, he was comfortable in a subordinate position, serving in any role the pastor needed. His training to fulfill God's plan ultimately came from experience and the lessons the four pastors he served taught him.

His first pastor became sandpaper on the arrogance of a new convert. With kindness and compassion, he taught George to listen to other opinions and be teachable. The second pastor instilled administrative skills and respect for the house of God. His third pastor taught him the importance of people skills and to temper his zeal for God. George's fourth pastor taught him to embrace change and a willingness to try new things—a lesson he greatly needed when God severed him from a thirty-year relationship with Christian Life Center.

The foundation for launching a new church began when a young lady George had known since she was a toddler asked him to officiate her wedding. George didn't have the necessary credentials. The wedding date made obtaining credentials from the Assemblies of God impossible. He contacted an independent full gospel organization that could qualify him before the wedding. To fulfill the requirements through the independent organization, he had to charter his church.

George looked thoughtful as he continued his story. "I didn't have a church. It was my goal to perform a wedding, not start a church. I prayed and jotted down some potential names, then crumpled the paper and tossed it in the trash. 'Amazing Love,' a popular song at the time, came to mind. I thought, *Wow, what an awesome name.* Church is all about God's amazing love." George charted the church in name only so he could perform the wedding.

Several years later, the Zancas became restless and sensed their time at Christian Life Center had come to an end. When his term as deacon ended, he withdrew his name for future consideration and stopped attending services. George and Jody agreed that it was time to leave but did not know where to go. As they waited for God's direction, Jody dressed for church on Sunday mornings and sat in their living room while George preached to his congregation of one.

Desiring fellowship with other believers, the Zancas attended their presbyter's Tuesday night Bible study at Hope Chapel. One night, Rev. Newfield taught about the God of a second chance. George listened intently to the story of a successful businessman who refused to answer a call to ministry. Finally, when he was sixty years old, the man yielded his life to God, and God used him to plant four churches. Rev. Newfield concluded his message, saying, "God never removes a calling. When you answer, he will fulfill his purpose for your life."

On the way home, George looked at Jody. "Do you think God is saying something to me?"

Jody responded with wisdom. "What do you think? Is God talking to you?"

"I'm not sixty, but I'm getting close. I'll have to pray about it."

God answered George's prayer when Rev. Newfield asked George if he had ever thought about starting a church. "I had thought about it, but not in the truest sense," said George. "I'd only pondered what it would be like to start a church but never intended to pursue it. Jody and I talked and decided to take steps to that end. At my age, there is no more pride. If I make a mistake, it's no big deal. I believe God is gracious, and he would put me back on the right path if I took a wrong turn by starting a church."

Rev. Newfield gave the Zancas permission to hold their first service on April 18, 2010, at Hope Chapel. The Zancas sent letters to friends and family who were not established in a church announcing the service. Forty people attended. The next week, twenty-eight returned, the week after that twenty-five, and George wondered if the congregation would decline to zero. It didn't. At the fourth service, attendance rose to thirty, then thirty-two, forty, fifty, and then settled to a consistent average of sixty-five.

Jody smiled and affirmed what George now knows. "I always knew George had a call on his life, and it wasn't going to stop at being a deacon. He didn't think he could be a pastor because he lacked education. I always told George it's not what you can do. It's what God can do through you."

God's Gift to the Ninth Ward

Pastor Reiger called me shortly after she was elected to the position of secretary-treasurer for the New Orleans Section Assembly of God. She planned to start a website as a communications hub for ministers and wanted me to write their profiles. "Start with Robert Burnside," she said. I've never regretted accepting her offer. Ministers always amaze me with the most remarkable stories.

Robert never met his father, and his older brother was in prison. He imitated the men in his neighborhood who made their livelihood preying on the misery of others. Robert realized he could become an addict or a dealer. Preferring profits over the pleasure drugs offered, he chose to be a dealer. By the time he dropped out of school, he had developed a profitable illegal drug business and thought he had found the easy way to wealth.

His lavish lifestyle screeched to a halt when he found himself staring through prison bars, feeling remorse for the lifestyle he chose. He had been charged with murder and faced a million-dollar bond. His future looked bleak until he remembered the stories his mother had told him about God's miraculous power. Hopeful God would do the same for him, he prayed for a miracle.

Unbeknown to Robert, God was already at work. While he waited in the holding tank, a prisoner was reassigned to the fourth floor of the prison to share a cell with Robert. Ricky taught a Bible study for the prisoners. Robert attended the study and also attended services held by the prison chaplain. Week after week, Robert marveled when the prison chaplain preached the same things Ricky taught in his Bible study.

One night Robert dreamed the police were chasing him in a rainstorm. Wet and frightened, he banged on the door of his home, pleading with his mother to let him in. His mother hollered through the door, "I'm not letting you in until you're ready to serve God."

Robert screamed, "I want to serve God." His mother opened the door. He stumbled into the house, pleading with God to forgive him, and wept as he felt the power of God course through his body, breaking the bondages in his life. Robert awoke, and then woke up Ricky and said, "I have to tell people about God. I have to tell everybody about God."

Ninety days later, God told Robert he would release him from prison. Robert told the other prisoners he was going home. They laughed and called him crazy. Thirty minutes later, the prisoners who derided Robert watched in amazement when the sheriff came to Robert's cell door and announced, "Burnside, you are leaving today." Robert walked into freedom wearing borrowed pants, a shirt three sizes too small, and slippers. He immediately called his lawyer, who had no knowledge of his release, confirming Robert's conviction that God had given him a second chance.

Teena Myers

Robert's friends quickly organized a block party to celebrate his release. As he watched his friends drinking and smoking weed, he knew that he no longer belonged among them. They offered him drugs and money. He took the much-needed cash, returned the drugs, and spoke frankly. "When we ran together, I was down with you, wasn't I?" said Robert. His friends agreed that he had always dealt with them honestly. Robert continued, "The same way I was with you, I'm gonna be with God."

As he stood to leave, one of his friends called out, "You'll be back."

When his former friends realized Robert wasn't coming back, a hit was ordered. He was filling up his gas tank at a Shell station when a man approached him. "Robert," the stranger said, "I took the hit on you. I don't know what it is, but I'm not going to kill you." As Robert watched the man walk away, he was overcome with the reality of a living God who had spared his life.

Robert didn't know how to fulfill his call to ministry. The answer came when he purchased flowers for his wife and the florist gave him a video about the School of Urban Missions (SUM). Robert enrolled in the Bible College. The following year, the chancellor of SUM called Robert with a message: "God wants you to help us establish a School of Urban Missions in California." Robert wasn't convinced the message was from God until the chancellor said, "He also wants you to get out of debt, finish your education, and obtain ministry credentials." The chancellor named the goals Robert had written on sticky notes and had stuck on a wall in his home. His wife, Sherdren, loved New Orleans, but she couldn't deny the hand of God in the chancellor's message.

Six years later, God sent him back to New Orleans to help rebuild the city. "I thought it was a Nehemiah call to build spiritual walls," said Robert. When he helped his pregnant wife into the car for the long ride back to New Orleans, he didn't know his calling was literal as well as spiritual.

They arrived in New Orleans in July 2005. The following month, Sherdren gave birth to their third child. The ominous winds of Hurricane Katrina approached the city, the same morning Sherdren and newborn Bethany were released from the hospital. Robert was inundated with phone calls from friends in California telling him he had made a mistake and pleaded with him to return. He appreciated their concern but knew God had called him to New Orleans.

Robert found temporary housing for his family in Pennsylvania. When the flood waters subsided, he returned to New Orleans to repair their home and started a trucking service. In his spare time, he assisted church efforts to help those in need. When schools reopened, he started a ministry to youth in high schools. His high school ministry ended when he received a phone call from Journey Fellowship Northshore.

A benefactor had purchased a damaged Lutheran church in the Ninth Ward of New Orleans and donated it to Journey Fellowship. The chancellor of SUM recommended Robert as the pastor. Robert accepted the position. He had everything necessary to conduct a church service except a congregation.

Robert started his day making repairs to the church and then walked the streets of the community sharing his faith. He transformed the corner drug dealers gathered to sell their wares into a Bible study. Week after week, he told them about the power of a living God who heals shattered lives. One evening, Robert walked to the corner to conduct his self-made Bible study. Everyone was gone. The unrepentant drug peddlers had been driven out of his community with the love of God.

Whenever Robert saw the police questioning someone in his community, he asked the officers if he could help. One day an officer told him, "We don't really want this guy. We want his buddy, Chucky. He has killed several people." The next time he saw Chucky, he requested a private meeting. Chucky's gang laughed at Robert, and Chucky brushed him off with a hollow promise.

Weeks later, Robert was about to conclude his sermon when he saw his congregation scrambling to clear a path. Chucky walked to the front of the church and said, "Pastor, I want to talk to you." Robert stopped his service and met Chucky at the altar. "I gotta get it right," said Chucky. Robert shared the gospel and prayed with Chucky to accept Christ as his Savior. Three days later, Chucky was murdered.

Pastor Robert reminded me of the messengers in the parable of the wedding banquet (Matthew 22:1-14). Jesus said the kingdom of heaven is like a king who prepared a wedding banquet and then sent messengers to call those who had been invited to the celebration. When the messengers were ignored and abused, the king destroyed the city but he didn't abandon it. He sent more messengers. New Orleans was destroyed by Hurricane Katrina but not abandoned. There is a messenger walking the streets of the Ninth Ward with an invitation from God.

A Shiny Pebble

I initially met Dr. Kathy Baker when a friend invited me to her monthly interfaith Bible study. It is impossible to accept every invitation I receive and politely declined. The next day, another friend called. "Teena, Pat and I are going to a Bible study led by Kathy Baker on Saturday. You wanna come with us?" When something repeatedly comes to my attention, I know God is leading. Carol parked her car in front of Longue Vue House and Gardens. We walked into the beautiful setting and listened to an intriguing message. At the conclusion of the study, Dr. Baker consented to tell me her story.

C. A. Beason paced the hospital waiting room anxious for news. His wife's pregnancy was fraught with difficulties. She had already lost two babies, and he didn't want to lose another one. A somber doctor walked into the waiting room. C. A. braced for bad news.

"You'll have to choose," said the doctor, "your wife or your baby."

He couldn't choose. "Where is the chapel?"

C. A. was no stranger to the things of God. His father was a Methodist preacher, and his wife had converted to Christianity. Disillusioned by the hypocrisy he witnessed in church, he had abandoned his father's God and wasn't interested in embracing his wife's faith. But his circumstance demanded help from a higher power. He sat in the dimly lit chapel and made a deal with God. "If you will give me my wife and my child, I'll give you the rest of my life."

He walked back to the waiting room, pondering what to tell the doctor. The doctor met him in the hall. "I don't know what happened, but your wife and baby girl are fine." C. A. named the daughter he had always wanted "Kathy." God had given him two lives for one and then balanced the deal by calling Kathy to serve him before she was born (Galatians 1:15).

"All I knew were Christian parents who loved God and me," said Kathy. "I knew that I was called to preach the gospel at a young age. In everything I did, God exalted me. I was the shiny pebble."

Kathy adored her father, who was larger than life in her eyes. He always told her that she could do anything she wanted to do until Kathy shared her calling. Kathy and her father were returning home after a Wednesday night service about missionaries. She looked at her father and said, "One day I'm going to preach the gospel." Her father rested his hand on his beloved daughter's shoulder and said, "Honey, I know you are very special, but girls don't do that."

Kathy's perfect world crumbled when her father barely survived triple bypass surgery. He returned home frail; months elapsed before he could walk. His brush with death made eight-year-old Kathy aware of the need to secure her eternal future. She had always communed with God through her music but felt prompted to do more. She yielded her life to God and asked to be baptized in water.

The following year, Kathy awoke to her mother's cries of pain. "Find your father; I'm sick." Kathy ran outside in her pajamas to find her father, who arose early to walk around the block for exercise. Still weak from his surgery, her father found the strength to run home and call the doctor. Kathy stood in the hall and watched her mother wheeled out of the house on a gurney and into the waiting ambulance. That was the last time she saw her mother alive.

"All of a sudden, my whole life was upside down. My mother was gone. My father slipped into a deep depression and became emotionally detached. In the middle of school, I would close my books and walk home. My nine-year-old mind reasoned I was in a bad dream. If I went home, everything would be different. Finally, my father threatened to put me in a boarding school if I couldn't control my behavior. Even though he was very compassionate, I felt rejected. Instead of boarding school, he enrolled me in Mid City Baptist. It was the best thing he could have done for me. I survived by burying myself in church activities."

Kathy did well in her new school, and her life was returning to normal when her father remarried. His new wife was insecure in their relationship and jealous of her husband's love for Kathy. She made the next five years of Kathy's life a hellish nightmare. Separated from her father's help by her stepmother's deception, Kathy longed for the day she could leave. Five days after graduating from high school, Kathy moved to Hattiesburg, Mississippi, to attend William Carey University. "My sudden departure broke my father's heart. He was never aware of the troublesome relationship I had with my stepmother. I had to leave to survive. This time I coped with life by burying myself in college activities."

During her sophomore year, Kathy's father was diagnosed with cancer. Radical surgery at Boston General Hospital's Cancer Center failed. He was fading fast by the end of her sophomore year. "His looming death was more than I could handle, so I enrolled in the summer semester to avoid going home," said Kathy. "My brother came to the college and warned me if I didn't come home, I'd never see him alive again."

Kathy didn't recognize the man resting in the recliner when she returned home. Her "General," as she affectionately called him, the man she adored who could do anything, was thin and frail. She spent every waking moment with him for two weeks. The night before he died, he called her to his bedside with the nickname he gave her. "Doodie Doll, I've got two things to tell you. One, you can do anything you want in this life if you want it enough. Two, don't ever forget that I love you."

Kathy hugged him. "I'll see you in the morning, Daddy." Her brother entered to sit with him, and Kathy went upstairs. Her father died at 5:00 a.m. the next morning.

"My brother decided a trip would help me deal with my grief, so I went to Corpus Christi to visit friends. Three days later, my sister-in-law called. My brother had died. I returned home to bury a third family member. Life didn't make sense. I was an orphan, and now my brother was gone. Then I returned home for Christmas. I came downstairs for church in the same dress I wore to my father's funeral. My stepmother flew into a rage when she saw the dress. She ordered me to change clothes and then demanded me to move out of the house. I had no place to go, and I was scared."

Kathy put her clothes and jewelry in the cream-yellow Monte Carlo her father bought her shortly before he died. She knew no one would be at the college, but having no place else to go, she headed for Hattiesburg. Tears streamed down her face as she pulled onto I-10 east. When she saw the exit for Read Boulevard, she remembered Word of Faith, the church her brother and sister-in-law attended. She had met Pastor Charles Green at her brother's funeral. It was Sunday; she was dressed for church, so she pulled into the parking lot.

The service had already started when Kathy walked through the wooden double doors. "The decision to visit Word of Faith changed my life. The instant I heard the worship, I knew I was home. To me, God is in music. That is where I find him and know him best," said Kathy. By the end of the service, Kathy knew she needed to stay in New Orleans.

"I was twenty-one when Pastor Green preached a message that redirected my life. My Baptist training taught me women can't preach the gospel, but I couldn't deny the calling tugging at my heart. In the sermon, Pastor Green explained that knowing we had a calling wasn't enough. We had to surrender to that calling. I met with Pastor Green the next day to explain that I had always known I had a calling. He leaned back in his chair and cracked up laughing as only Charles Green can do. Then he said, 'I was wondering when you were going to figure that out.' He didn't tell me I couldn't do it. He didn't tell me I was crazy. He believed me. I enrolled in Word of Faith's Bible College."

Pastor Myrtle D. Beall, the founder and pastor of Bethesda Missionary Temple in Detroit, Michigan, was the first woman minister Kathy met. Affectionately known as Mom Beall, she spoke regularly at Word of Faith. Kathy went to the altar for prayer after one of her sermons. Pastor Beall looked at Kathy and said, "Oh my! Who are you? You are very special." Then she turned and said to Pastor Green standing behind her, "Charles, she is very special." Pastor Green nodded in agreement.

Pastor Beall became Kathy's mentor and unraveled decades of teaching that women can't preach the gospel. They talked by phone for months. Whenever Pastor Green's family went to Detroit for a convention, they brought Kathy with them.

"Pastor Beall knew the kind of resistance I would face," said Kathy. "There was a glass ceiling I had to break through. I was a keynote speaker at a worship conference in Dallas with a thousand in attendance. The man who spoke before me started with scripture in Genesis and went to Revelation, explaining why women should not be in ministry. You could have cut the tension with a knife. By the time he finished, I wondered if I had erred when I entered the ministry. I went to my hotel room in tears and called my husband. He prayed for me and encouraged me to do what I do best. The man who introduced me at the next session said, 'Well, you have to admit that any woman who has the courage to stand up here now deserves a standing ovation.' Everyone in the audience stood up and cheered."

A woman in ministry is a controversial issue in the church. I've learned to resolve difficult questions by comparing the words attributed to man in the Bible with the "thus saith the Lord" scriptures. Micah chapter 6 begins "Listen to what the Lord says..." The Lord listed the good things he had done for Israel. First item on the list, he brought Israel out of Egypt. Second item, "I sent Moses to lead you, also Aaron and Miriam." Clearly, God sent three people to lead Israel, two men and a woman. That one statement from God trumps all scriptures that appear to deny women a place of leadership.

Never Too Old

After I started writing NOLA's faith blog, my family returned to a church where I had taught a Sunday school class. Several of my former students still attended the church, among them Betty Burke. Betty, still actively serving her Lord at eighty-two years of age, had started a Bible study at the retirement complex where she lived. She invited me to speak. I jotted down the address.

Walkers were parked in the corner of the conference room when I arrived. The table overflowed with Catholic, Baptist, Presbyterian, Methodist, Lutheran, and Pentecostal women. Before I left, I collected fodder for NOLA's faith blog.

Betty found salvation in a Baptist church sitting at her grandmother's feet. She was active in home missions work when her pastor received the baptism in the Holy Spirit and changed his doctrine. Much to Betty's dismay, many in the congregation joined the pastor in this new experience. "I was the last one to receive the baptism in the Spirit and speak with other tongues because I was too busy trying to prove they were wrong," said Betty.

When Baptist authorities learned of the mission's departure from their acceptable doctrine, they asked the wayward members to leave. Betty and her friends tried to join the Pentecostals. The women in their disenfranchised congregation wore makeup, and the Pentecostals didn't want them either. Without a home to call its own, the group quickly flourished into an independent church. During this time, Betty became an ordained minister and traveled extensively, preaching the Word of God.

Betty desired to be a missionary, but after her children were grown and she entered her fifties, it appeared the time for missionary work had passed. It hadn't. When Betty turned sixty, the door opened for her to preach the gospel in Japan. Her missionary work was cut short when she returned to America and discovered her mother in poor health.

After Betty's mother went home to be with the Lord, she moved to a retirement complex and joined a church near the apartments. She sought to resume her ministry work, but the church did not have a place of service for her. While Betty visited with her friends Bernice and Pauline, the subject of a Bible study to meet the needs of the residents arose. Without knowledge of Betty's background in ministry, Bernice and Pauline decided Betty should teach.

They initially met in the foyer near Betty's apartment. Pauline left to live with family shortly after the study began. Betty and Bernice continued the work, which quickly outgrew the tiny foyer, so the small congregation moved to the community room. "Many of the residents led productive lives before entering the retirement apartments and wrestle with depression as they adjust to a new way of life," said Betty. In addition to teaching, Betty and Bernice care for their flock by visiting them when they are in the hospital or are too ill to leave their apartments.

Teena Myers

Betty and Bernice reminded me of Moses and Aaron, who found the fulfillment of their calling in their eighties. No one can accuse God of age discrimination. Whether we are eight or eighty-eight, he has a place of service for everyone with a willing heart.

Faith, Trust, and Reason

Rod, my husband, suggested I attend the Louisiana Book Festival, a literary celebration offering book lovers an opportunity to interact with authors. I suggested he bring me. We strolled through the grounds of the state capital, weaving our way through a maze of tables stacked with books overseen by authors ready to tell us about their labors of love. By mid-afternoon, the weather grew warm. We headed toward a tent to escape the sun's beating rays. Within the tent were more tables, books, and authors.

Wishing to remain in the shade, we took our time at each table. I stopped to peruse the back cover of *Walk Back the Cat* (rereleased in 2010 as *Secret of the Shroud*). Pamela Binnings Ewen stood, waiting patiently, as I read "Walk Back the Cat is an intense fictional work based upon actual details of a real artifact, *The Shroud of Turin*, the purported burial cloth of Jesus." Jesus interested me. Fiction did not.

Pamela handed me a copy of *Faith on Trial*, a nonfiction book she wrote to prove the Gospel accounts of Jesus's life and resurrection are creditable evidence acceptable in a court of law. I looked at my husband. No words needed. He fished his wallet out of his back pocket. I walked out of the tent with my book and a new friend in Pamela. Four years later, I asked Pamela if I could write about her experience in Christianity.

Pamela's family attended the Catholic Church but remained detached from its activities. She loved the mystery of a mass spoken in Latin, the rituals, the incense, and the candles. When she was in the fourth grade, her family moved to a small town in south Louisiana, where the Episcopal Church became the center of their lives. Pamela studied the Bible in Sunday school, sang in the choir, and most of her friends attended the church's youth group. During Christmas, they cut down pine trees and decorated the inside of the church.

Pamela smiled. "To this day, the smell of pine boughs reminds me of the time I spent in the Episcopal Church. I loved the priest. The congregation became my family. Going to church was comfortable, like being at home. I lost that when I went to college."

Pamela moved to New Orleans to attend college. Far from the watchful eyes of her parents and priest, she was intoxicated by the lure of the big city. Swept up in the party atmosphere New Orleans is known for, Pamela flunked her first year of college. She walked off the campus with "you are not college material" ringing in her ears and looked for a job.

While working in New Orleans, Pamela found a new moral compass, Ayn Rand. Rand's books and philosophy were powerful arguments against religion. The objectivism preached by Rand gave Pamela strong reasons to believe the Bible was little more than a collection of myths and legends. Daily newscast of wars, starvation in Africa, and irreconcilable differences in the Middle East made believing in a man who rose from the dead to bring peace on earth unreasonable. Pamela wondered if the Bible was little more than the skillful spinning of gifted storytellers. Every ancient religion had a great flood, virgin births, and resurrected gods.

Unwilling to abandon her faith, she asked her childhood pastor, "How do you know the Gospel story of Jesus is true?" She hoped for a persuasive argument proving Jesus lived, died, and rose from the dead. His reply, "faith based on trust," left her disappointed and disillusioned.

As Pam searched for answers, *Time* magazine came out with a cover story titled "Is God Dead?" The article pushed Pamela toward agnosticism. By the end of the 1960s, Pamela returned to college to study law. She graduated Cum Laude, married an atheist, and strived to acquire the best life had to offer.

"My heart could not accept what my mind rejected," said Pamela. "I asked God to show me something that would help me believe. When I moved to Houston to practice law, I'd often skip lunch to attend a healing service in a small Episcopal Chapel. The priest would lay his hand on my head while I closed my eyes, wanting to believe. Sometimes I cried. God seemed to remain silent, and I descended deeper into agnosticism."

Many years elapsed before a thought slipped into Pamela's consciousness and refused to leave. What is the meaning of life if this is all there is? She loved practicing law, problem solving, traveling, and working with people she admired. But her success could not quiet the question that distracted her in noisy, crowded conference rooms and pursued her as she ran through airports to catch a plane. She was able to dismiss the unanswerable question until her father died. The idea that death was the end and that her father was nothing more than dust tormented her.

"One day I gazed at the bookshelves in my office filled with thick, gold embossed leather binders, each one representing months, even years, of my life. One by one, I took them down and checked the dates. Suddenly, I realized everything that I'd accomplished as a lawyer was temporary—concerns that drove these deals would abate, become outdated. Contracts would be modified, terminated, replaced with new agreements to be negotiated and written by new lawyers. Goals would change. Friends, partners, and clients would come and go. As Solomon tells us in Ecclesiastes, 'Yet when I surveyed all that my hands had done and what I had toiled to achieve, everything was meaningless…'"

The depiction of Mozart in the movie *Amadeus* made Pamela think there may be something more than this life. His childish behavior contradicted the genius of his music. She read everything that she could find about Mozart for an explanation. The superficial, scatological man she found in *Mozart's Letters, Mozart's Life* made Pamela wonder if his talent came from a higher power.

"I also began reading books by scientists discussing their thoughts about God. After ten years of research, I decided it was probable that consciousness is not limited to our physical brain. There is more to life than we see, feel, and touch, something that continues beyond our physical lives. But I wasn't ready to embrace Christianity yet."

Pamela turned her attention to the Bible after she read *Testimony of the Evangelist* by Simon Greenleaf. Greenleaf, a famous professor of law at Harvard in the mid-1800s, wrote the first rules of evidence for lawyers in the United States. In *Testimony of the Evangelist*, Greenleaf treated Matthew, Mark, Luke, and John, the authors of the Gospels, as witnesses in a courtroom, subjecting them to the rigorous test of law. His examination of the witnesses' testimony led to the conclusion that they were reliable, credible. Therefore, it was reasonable to believe that the resurrection did in fact happen. Pamela also realized that now, 150 years after Greenleaf published his conclusions, a new test using current archeological and scientific discoveries might make his case stronger.

"The realization that Matthew, Mark, Luke, and John were witnesses and I could use the rules of evidence to test their claims was manna from heaven. I don't have to listen to my heart or believe what someone told me scripture said. We have four books that are unique. There's no other religion in the world that claims to have witnesses whose stories are tied to historical events. We can tie history to the evidence found in the Gospels. One thing leads to the next, and the next, and the next, and before you know it, you have a chain of proof that makes believing the gospels reasonable. It's easy to tell if someone is telling the truth when you have enough evidence. I decided to turn my research into a book that became *Faith on Trial*."

Before Pamela finished her manuscript, she returned to church and immersed herself in its community. Her atheist husband refused to attend services with her and forbade her from bringing church friends home. Her drive to complete *Faith on Trial* became a point of contention in their marriage. She already worked long hours as a lawyer, and her free time was increasingly consumed with writing and church activities. Their marriage deteriorated until divorce became the only option.

Pamela began writing as an agnostic but completed her manuscript as a woman of faith. She lay on a hospital bed battling cancer when an unfamiliar priest wearing the collar of the Episcopal clergy walked into the room. "I'm miserable," she said to the priest. He smiled and handed her a publishing contract for *Faith on Trial*. Pamela survived her battle with cancer and later wrote *The Moon and the Mango Tree*, a novel based on her grandmother's search for faith in the 1920s. The book became a 2009 Christy Award Finalist.

She looked at me and spoke with confidence. "I remember reading Ayn Rand as a young woman in the sixties. It was so powerful, but I really didn't want to give up my faith. I wanted someone to say, 'Faith doesn't conflict with reason.' That's why apologetics is the root of all my writing. Fiction is more fun, and it may even be a stronger tool than a head-on confrontation. But my core being, the center of everything I do in life is in *Faith on Trial*. My faith is solid now because

I have reason to believe Matthew, Mark, Luke, and John told the truth."

While I don't usually read fiction, I have read all of Pamela's. Her love for apologetics is something I identify with. To believe something without a good reason is foolish. When Jesus said we must become like children to enter the kingdom of heaven, he wasn't talking about blind faith that trusts without reason. My husband has worked in children's ministry for thirty years. Set a child in an unfamiliar place, and he or she will scream to return to the comfort of someone they know. In the same way, our faith should be in someone we know and have a reason to believe we can trust.

Fit for Service

Elizabeth Garcia-Smith accepted Christ on Easter Sunday when she was eleven years old. Three years later, her mother stopped attending church. "I had to take two buses through dangerous neighborhoods to get to the church," said Elizabeth. When daylight savings started, I was afraid to ride the bus at night, so I stopped going too. But the desire to be in the presence of God never left me. During high school and my first year at college, I occasionally attended mass at a Catholic church near my home, but I wasn't committed to following Christ."

Elizabeth had lived at home during her first year of graduate school, but the commute proved difficult. The following year, she decided to live on campus. A white bookcase and Bible written in Korean and English was waiting in front of the door to her suite when she arrived. "My roommates told me the items belonged to the former occupant and I could keep them. I attended church with my Presbyterian roommate, but I remained uncommitted to following Christ."

Elizabeth graduated with a master's degree in dance education and accepted a position with the New York Board of Education. She loved her job and thought she would spend the rest of her life teaching. As 1997 drew near its end, Elizabeth heard a voice in the depths of her soul say, "I want to draw you back to me." Recognizing the voice as God's, she made a New Year's resolution to return to Bethlehem Church, where she had made a commitment to follow Christ when she was eleven.

"The first Sunday in 1998, I walked into the church and said to God, 'I'm here.'" This time Elizabeth was serious about fulfilling her commitment. As she spent more time in God's presence, the gentle voice of the Holy Spirit led her to make changes. "Changing the way I lived was difficult but not a struggle. Anything the Holy Spirit convicted me about was gone with no looking back."

Nine months later, Elizabeth attended a women's ministry conference. Reverend Joan Millar spoke about her work at the School of Urban Missions (SUM) in New Orleans, Louisiana. "When Reverend Millar spoke about the school, my heart leaped within me," said Elizabeth. "I didn't pursue attending the school, but there was a connection that I could not deny."

More than a year later, Reverend Millar returned to speak at a Women's Ministry Spring Rally for the City of New York. After the service, Elizabeth approached the altar for prayer. Reverend Millar's prayer confirmed to Elizabeth that God had called her to ministry. Before she left the rally, Elizabeth stopped at the SUM booth to pick up a packet of information about the school.

"The packet lay unopened on my desk for three months," said Elizabeth. "I attempted to open it several times but stopped. I knew the moment I opened that envelope I'd have to deal with the reality of leaving everything to fulfill the calling God had placed on my life."

Elizabeth became restless and no longer desired to teach her class. She sought God for a solution to the unhappiness in her life. God revealed that he was preparing her for ministry. Uncertain that the revelation was from God, she challenged him to prove that he was speaking to her. "I was vice president of the women's ministry at Bethlehem Church and scheduled to speak at the next meeting. Before I left, I prayed, 'God, if I'm really called to ministry, I want Sister Bea to lay hands on me, speak in tongues, and then prophesy that you have called me to full-time ministry.'"

At the end of the service, Elizabeth saw Sister Bea walking toward the exit and said, "Okay, Lord, I guess I'm not going to SUM." Suddenly, Sister Bea turned around, walked to the altar, and stood in front of Elizabeth. She laid hands on her, spoke in tongues, and prophesied that God had called Elizabeth to full-time ministry. That night Elizabeth opened the packet of information from SUM and filled out the admission form.

"I had taken the first step, but the battle wasn't over. I didn't want to leave New York. Then my boyfriend proposed and slipped the engagement ring on my finger. After he left, I wept and promised God I would go to SUM next year," said Elizabeth.

A friend who had been present for Sister Bea's prophesy learned Elizabeth returned to her teaching job and confronted her. "What happened to SUM?" said Eileen.

"I'll go next year. I'm still teaching, and I'm getting married—"

"Excuse me," Eileen interrupted. "You asked God about this. He gave you the answer, and you're just gonna brush him off like that? You call SUM as soon as you wake up tomorrow, and I'm gonna call to see if you did."

Early Monday morning, the phone woke Elizabeth. Eileen demanded to know if she had called SUM yet. Irritated and convinced Eileen would not leave her alone until she called, Elizabeth dialed the number to SUM. Reverend Joan Millar answered. Elizabeth explained how she came to the conviction God had called her to attend the school.

"If you know you belong here, you better get on the plane this week," said Reverend Millar. "We are in the second week of school, but I'll approve your application if you arrive before Thursday."

"What am I gonna do about my bills?" said Elizabeth.

"You can work at McDonalds."

"McDonalds! I'm a teacher."

"You can waitress at the Holiday Inn."

"That's not gonna pay my bills. I've already committed to teach another year. I can't pull out at the last minute."

"If God wants you at SUM, the principal will release you from your commitment without any complications."

The conversation with Reverend Millar pricked Elizabeth at the core of her being. "The next three days were agony," said Elizabeth. "By Tuesday evening, I'd made up my mind to attend SUM. Then I talked to my fiancé and changed my mind. Wednesday morning, Eileen called to find out if I'd bought a ticket to New

Orleans yet. I told her, 'I'm not going,' hung up the phone, and then fell on my face begging God to tell me one more time that I was called to full-time ministry."

A battle raged for Elizabeth's soul as she cried all morning and into the afternoon. The struggle ceased when she heard God say, "Today, choose who you will serve. If you choose me, I'll be faithful to you and you will fulfill the calling on your life." Elizabeth wiped the tears from her eyes and called the principal to see if she could be released from her teaching commitment. Reverend Millar's counsel proved prophetic. The principal released her with a blessing. Elizabeth purchased an airline ticket and left her career, family, friends, and fiancé. She arrived in New Orleans fully committed to follow Christ.

Elizabeth's story produced a new respect in me for ministers. I didn't realize how difficult it is to give up everything and follow a calling. God rewarded her obedience with a new fiancé that she met while attending the School of Urban Missions. After they married, they accepted a pastorate in New Orleans and then lost everything, including their congregation, in Hurricane Katrina. Fully committed to their calling, they remained to rebuild their church and minister to the needs of a suffering city.

God's Shepherds

I dialed Tawanna Gross's phone number. Pastor Thomas, her husband, answered. He handed the phone to Tawanna. They were out of town. She asked me to call back the following week. Again, Thomas answered the phone. He gave me Tawanna's cell phone number. For the next month, I played phone tag with Tawanna. Pastor Thomas was easier to connect with, so I called and scheduled an interview with him and Tawanna, if she was available. The following week, I knocked on the door of Living Faith Christian Fellowship. Tawanna answered and told me I could interview both of them.

"My mother was eighteen when she conceived me in an adulterous relationship," said Thomas. "A family member advised her to get an abortion, so she drank some stuff that was supposed to abort me. All it did was make her sick. My mother's sister was childless and agreed to take me if I was a girl. When I was born, my aunt said she didn't want a 'nappy-headed' boy."

After giving birth to two more sons, Thomas's mother told her sister that she might never have a girl so she might as well take Thomas. Thomas's aunt decided a boy wasn't so bad and took him to live with her in Los Angeles.

"I called her 'Mommy,' and she loved me as her son, but I knew she wasn't my real mother," said Thomas.

Thomas's aunt, a devout Baptist, brought him to church every Sunday. While attending Sunshine

Finding Faith in the City Care Forgot

Missionary Baptist Church, Thomas walked to the altar with tears streaming down his face. He didn't remember what brought him to the altar that day, but he never forgot what his pastor said: "Thomas, I'm gonna turn you into a preacher." The pastor's desire was thwarted when his aunt moved her membership to Bethesda Missionary Baptist Church.

"I didn't understand salvation until I was twelve years old and returned to New Orleans to visit my mother. She had stopped smoking and drinking beer. She read Revelation 21:8 to me: 'But the cowardly, the unbelieving, the vile, the murderers, the sexually immoral, those who practice magic arts, the idolaters and all liars—their place will be in the fiery lake of burning sulfur.' That was the first time I understood hell as a literal place," said Thomas. "Later that day, I thought about the things my mother told me and asked Jesus to forgive my sins. I returned to Los Angeles with my aunt, but my mother had the greatest influence on my life."

While Thomas grew into a young man in Los Angeles, Tawanna struggled to survive in a dysfunctional family. "I was a rebellious child," said Tawanna, "always getting suspended from school for fighting. I believe a lot of it stemmed from my dad's aggressive behavior. I could not stop him from beating my mother, so I took out my frustration on the students at school. My dad didn't want my mother to go to church, but she brought us anyhow. Her faith in God was a lifeline that held her together through difficult times."

As Tawanna entered her teenage years, her mother repeatedly told her, "If you give your life to the Lord, he will send a godly man to be your husband. If you don't, you might end up experiencing the same things I do with your dad." Their pastor, Reverend Percy Casberry, often supported and reinforced her mother's admonition.

By the time Tawanna reached fourteen, the desire to be a proper young lady replaced her aggressive behavior. One Sunday, her pastor preached a sermon about hell. "The Bible says the beginning of wisdom is to fear the Lord," said Tawanna, "and the message about hell put the fear of God in me. I committed my life to Christ, and God filled me with the Holy Spirit."

One day Tawanna stopped to shake her pastor's hand after a service. "Tawanna," said Pastor Casberry, "what kind of husband do you want?"

"I want a minister," said Tawanna.

"If God has to bring him all the way from Europe, he will bring a godly man to be your husband," replied Pastor Casberry. The pastor's declaration proved true. God had already brought Thomas back to New Orleans.

"I was sixteen when I returned to New Orleans," said Thomas. "Every time we visited my mother, my aunt asked me if I wanted to stay, and I had always said no. She was shocked when I said yes."

Thomas had strayed from God but dutifully attended the Church of God in Christ with his mother. Tawanna's pastor preached a revival in their church that prompted Thomas to rededicate his life to God. Tawanna smiled. "God used my pastor to prepare Thomas for me and prepared me to meet him in an unusual way. A prize in a box of Cracker Jacks included

Finding Faith in the City Care Forgot

a fortune that said 'You are going to meet a man named Thomas.' Before the month ended, I met Thomas at a concert."

"I almost didn't go to the concert," said Thomas. "I had been working in a cafeteria all day. The best clothes I had were the ones I was wearing, and I couldn't find my comb. My mother reminded me that I had made a promise to play the organ at the concert and that I needed to keep my promises. I grabbed a fork from the kitchen drawer to tame my afro and headed out the door. After the concert, I asked Tawanna for her phone number."

"God connected us that night," said Tawanna.

While Thomas and Tawanna were dating, God dealt with Thomas about ministry. "I had always felt there was a calling upon my life to be a pastor," said Thomas, "but I didn't want to force anything, so I fasted and prayed. One afternoon I said, 'Lord, I'm just a child. I can't do this.' That night Twanna's pastor preached at my church. He opened his Bible to Jeremiah chapter one and read: 'The word of the Lord came to me, saying, "Before I formed you in the womb I knew you, before you were born I set you apart; I appointed you as a prophet to the nations." "Ah, Sovereign Lord," I said, "I do not know how to speak; I am only a child." But the Lord said to me, "Do not say, 'I am only a child.' You must go to everyone I send you to and say whatever I command you."'

As Pastor Casberry read the scripture, Thomas knew God had called him to preach the gospel. Thomas and Tawanna married and immersed themselves in ministry. Tawanna led the choir. Thomas became a youth pastor. Each of them taught a Sunday school class.

"I was initially licensed in the Church of God in Christ," said Thomas, "but was denied ordination. My ministry had come to a stalemate. When I heard God was moving in a mighty way at an Assembly of God church in New Orleans, we decided to visit. We loved the service and discussed joining the church."

"It was hard for me to leave the church where I grew up," said Tawanna, "but Thomas prayed for me and committed the matter to God. I prayed until my heart was in agreement with Thomas's desire."

Thomas grinned. "At the Church of God in Christ, we felt like we were banging on a door that no one answered. The door was wide open in the Assemblies of God. I was licensed to preach when an assistant pastor approached me about a satellite church. I accepted oversight of the congregation and six months later became an ordained pastor."

When a decision was made to close the satellite churches, Thomas and his congregation took over the expenses and continued the work. The congregation grew, and they rented a bigger building. They were forced to move to a temporary location in a Methodist church when a restaurant purchased their building. Thomas learned that Living Faith Christian Fellowship needed a pastor, so he entered into negotiations to merge their congregations.

"It wasn't pretty," said Thomas. "Living Faith was bankrupt, and the abrupt resignation of its pastor had left a lot of people bitter."

"I was young and naive," said Tawanna. I was so excited about having a bigger church family. I wanted to hug and embrace everybody, but I could barely get a handshake."

"The next three years were difficult," Thomas continued the story. "I used to read about the children of Israel in the wilderness and wonder why they were so hard to deal with. I saw the same things in my congregation and concluded that people are the same in every generation. But I learned to be patient and saw some of the most difficult people become the best Christians."

"I began to seek God like I never had before and had a supernatural encounter," said Tawanna. "It was my habit to pray after my children left for school. One morning, I noticed a book on my husband's desk titled *Ordinary Christian*. I thumbed through the book to get a flavor of its message and then went to the sanctuary and said, 'Lord, I don't want to be an ordinary Christian. I'm not leaving until I know you better.' As soon as I started to pray, a tingling sensation came over me and then a weighty feeling and uncontrollable weeping. I remember being on my back and thought I was having a heart attack. I stood up to go to Thomas's office and felt like I was wading through a pool of water. When I reached his office, my hand was heavy and trembling so much I had difficulty opening the door. I told Thomas what happened, and he motioned for me to return to the altar. When I reached the sanctuary, I heard a voice say, 'It's me,' and then I heard 'I am anointing you to worship me, to preach my Word and to be a better help for your husband.'"

I had intended to write a separate article about Thomas and Tawanna. As the conversation progressed, it became clear that I needed to write one article. Their lives exhibit God's plan for marriage from the beginning of time. "The Lord God said, 'It is not good for the man to be alone. I will make a helper suitable for him'" (Genesis 2:18). Clearly, God had prepared Thomas and Tawanna to labor together in ministry.

He Hasn't Failed Me Yet

I met Ellen Brown at a ministers meeting. At one time we attended the same church but never had occasion to become acquainted. As we chatted during lunch, I was impressed with her confidence and strength.

"My husband promised he would never cheat on me again, and he kept his word. The next time he found someone new, he moved out," said Ellen.

An intercessor at Ellen's church told her it was time to separate from her husband. Ellen felt only God had the right to dissolve her marriage. She prayed, "God, if you want me to separate myself from my husband, you will have to separate my husband from my heart." Ten days later, Ellen realized she had stopped praying for her husband's restoration. When she received divorce papers, she agreed to the dissolution of their marriage.

While attending a prayer conference, Ellen saw a vision of a seaport. She left the conference with the conviction that God had called her to missions. Later that year, she took a group tour to Israel and searched in vain for the seaport she saw in her vision. The following year, she felt a growing burden to pray for the city of New Orleans. It never occurred to Ellen that New Orleans is a port city. For the next three years, she continued searching for the seaport she saw in her vision.

Ash Wednesday 1974, Ellen rummaged through a drawer for her camera when a picture of a seaport caught her attention. "There it is!" Ellen shouted. Snatching the picture from the drawer, she turned it over and read "New Orleans Tour Guide." Ellen fell across her bed, crying and praying, "If you want me there, you will just have to pick me up and put me there."

An hour later, she heard a still small voice say, "Call Teen Challenge New Orleans." Ellen had recently read an article about the opening of Teen Challenge, a faith-based drug rehabilitation program, in New Orleans. Ellen glanced at the clock—9:50 p.m. Even though it was late, she called the operator for a phone number. The operator gave her two numbers. She chose one and decided to forget about the vision if no one answered.

"New Orleans Teen Challenge," said a young man.

Before he could say another word, she rattled off, "My name is Ellen Brown. I live in Fort Smith, Arkansas, and would like to know how to apply as a secretary with your organization."

"As a what?"

"As a secretary."

"That's way out! Even for God, this is way out!" the young man exclaimed.

"What do you mean?" said Ellen.

"I was praying for a secretary when the phone rang!"

Ellen filled out the job application she received in the mail and then called Teen Challenge to inquire what she could bring with her. The director of the center informed her she would only have one medium-sized bedroom.

"I don't know if this is God's will or not," said Ellen. "God told me to bring my bedroom furniture and organ."

"You have an organ! We've been praying for an organ."

Convinced God had called her to New Orleans, Ellen mailed the application. The application lay on the front desk when the director's wife pointed at the attached picture and said to her husband, "That's her. That's the secretary God wants."

Ellen planned to pay off her bills before she left Fort Smith in October, but the Holy Spirit told her to be in New Orleans before April 21. The unplanned and abrupt departure left her with a financial problem. After fasting and praying, she promised God she wouldn't be too proud to accept a financial gift.

Ellen arrived in New Orleans on the evening of the twenty-first. During a conversation with one of the students, she shared how a deacon at her church in Arkansas had given her an application for credentials and told her to fill it out, but she had never submitted the application. When the dean of men learned from the student that Ellen still had the completed application, he invited her to attend a ministers meeting with him and told her to bring the application.

"The next morning, I was locking the door to my room and started to say, 'God, if you called me here, I have to have some financial help.' I'd only said, 'God, if' when the Holy Spirit asked me if I doubted that he had called me to New Orleans. I started crying and said, "No, I don't doubt that."

During the ministers meeting, a pastor approached Ellen and told her God had awakened him in the middle of the night to tell him that she needed financial help. Not only did Ellen receive the much-needed help, but the district officials at the meeting accepted her application for Christian Workers Papers that led to her ordination.

Ellen swallowed the last bite of her jambalaya and set her fork on the table. "New Orleans has been my home for thirty-three years now, and God hasn't failed me yet." She spoke with the conviction that comes from experience. When God calls us to ministry, he supplies our every need.

Devils Beware

As I focused my camera on Dr. Kathy Baker, she explained to the congregation that I had written an article about her ministry and planned to include a video of her teaching. My face flushed with embarrassment when she praised my writing. Little did I know that God was arranging a divine appointment.

During the Bible study, Janyce Stratton mentioned she had been a dancer on Bourbon Street. Immediately interested, I made a mental note to inquire if she would tell me how God brought her from Bourbon Street to Christianity. At the conclusion of the study, I sat next to Janyce and said, "I'd like to talk to you."

Tears spilled from her eyes, making tiny rivers down her cheeks. "I have stories to tell but I don't know how," Janyce sobbed. "I come from generations of witches. When I was a child, I thought it was normal to walk through cold spots, hear voices, and see household furnishings fly across the room. My mother told me they were friendly spirits and our gifts came from God."

Janyce had more than stories. She talked until the three-hour battery on my recorder died and then gave me a two-hundred page single-spaced manuscript detailing her encounters with devils, miraculous healings, and hilarious stories about street evangelism.

A bad marriage left Janyce stranded in New Orleans when she was seventeen. Lacking marketable job skills, Janyce applied for a job at the recently opened Playboy

Club on Iberville Street and became one of the first locals hired as a Playboy Bunny. Her Bunny career ended when she failed to master the Bunny Dip—a graceful backward arch used while serving drinks to keep breasts from popping out of the costume. Janyce's breast made an unwelcome appearance one too many times. She quit. Her next job, Bourbon Street dancer, opened the door to the mob's inner circle, and she descended into alcoholism.

By age thirty, Janyce's skin was yellow and gray. A doctor diagnosed her with cirrhosis of the liver, brain damage, leukemia, hypoglycemia, and syphilis. She left the doctor's office with a dire warning: stop drinking or die. Janyce joined Alcoholic Anonymous, but the longest she remained sober was six months.

Thinking a cure was impossible, Janyce tried to drown her sorrow in alcohol. She stumbled out of a barroom and into her car. "As my car barreled down the street, I suddenly found myself sitting in the passenger seat watching myself drive the car and thought I was crazy. I looked up and saw someone watching me from a cloud, and then I smashed into another car."

When the police arrived, Janyce fought with them. By the time they reached the jail, she was considered dangerous. The officer thrust her in the cell without removing the shackles from her arms and legs. Janyce received a second epiphany to her true state when a woman twice her size was thrust into the cell with her. As the woman stared at Janyce, fear crept over her face. She slowly backed toward the door and screamed for someone to let her out. The terror in the woman's voice brought an officer to the cell who removed the terrified woman.

In the silence that followed, a thought broke into her consciousness: "That woman was afraid of me." For the second time that night, Janyce realized that she needed help. Suddenly, she lost control of her bodily functions, and she saw her life pass before her. Then she heard a voice say, "You need Jesus."

"I'm a good servant of the devil. Why would Jesus help me?"

Again the voice said, "You need Jesus."

"What if I call on Jesus and he doesn't show up?"

Janyce wasn't sure if she was in her body or having an out-of-body experience when she saw hell and smelled burning flesh. At that point, she accepted it was her lot in life to spend eternity in hell and wept tears of regret.

For the third time, she heard, "You need Jesus."

Janyce paused, struggling to contain her emotions so she could continue her story. I sipped my tea, waiting patiently as Janyce's thoughts traveled back in time to a precious memory. "Teena," she said. "I didn't have anything to lose, so I looked up and said, 'Jesus.' That one word embodied my desperate plea for help." Janyce's chin quivered. Tears filled her eyes. "Jesus walked into my cell and showed me the scars on his hands and feet. He told me that I didn't have to die and then put his arms around me and said, 'I love you just the way you are.' All I ever wanted was someone to love me. After that, strange noises came out of me, and then I screamed so hard I couldn't breathe."

When Janyce stopped screaming, the cell door opened. An officer entered, removed the shackles, and helped her walk to a phone. Janyce called a friend to pick her up. She awoke the following morning and cried all day, positive that she would return to drugs and alcohol, but she never did. Later, she learned every disease the doctor had diagnosed her with was gone. Janyce readily acknowledged finding her way to a normal life took years. She learned to read listening to an audio recording of the Bible and comparing the words in her written Bible. Janyce worked her way through Bible school and started a street ministry. Every weekend she faithfully handed out gospel tracts at 500 Bourbon Street.

Having been raised in witchcraft, Janyce knew devils were real. While handing out gospel tracts, a man dressed in filthy clothes and ragged tennis shoes, laces dragging on the ground, shuffled toward her. Without looking at Janyce, he stuck his hand in her direction. "Give me twenty-five cents," he demanded. His words sounded as if they came from an echo chamber.

Fear gripped Janyce, but she refused to be intimidated. "Sir, I don't have any money."

A young kid dropped fifteen cents in his hand. "Now you only need a dime."

The man looked at his hand and then looked at Janyce. He closed his fingers around the money and said, "Who's driving the hearse?"

Janyce grabbed the man by the shoulders. "I know whose driving this body. I bind you, devil. Loose this man." As Janyce demanded the devil to leave, a curious crowd gathered.

"What is your name? I want to talk to the owner of this body," Janyce demanded.

A quiet, quivering voice said, "I'm Herman."

"Herman, how did you get like this?"

"A witch doctor put a curse on me." Herman's head snapped back and then forward. His bloodshot eyes glowed red like a car's taillights. A gruff voice said, "I'm the witch who put the curse on Herman."

"I don't want to talk to you!" Janyce snapped. "Herman, do you want to be free of this devil?"

"Yes," Herman's frail voice answered. As Janyce led him in prayer to forgive everyone who had hurt him, green mucus oozed from his mouth and nose.

Janyce chuckled. "It was like the movie *The Exorcist*. I prayed with him for a long time, and then Herman shuffled down the street. I never saw him again, but that experience changed my life. I realized the bondage unforgiveness, bitterness, and rebellion produce. I also acquired a reputation as a professional exorcist."

Janyce and her evangelism team were walking down Bourbon Street when a young girl with a long ponytail stopped her. "Can you help me get free from witchcraft?" Janyce and her team immediately began praying for the girl and binding devils in the name of Jesus.

"Leave me alone!" a high-pitched voice screamed. The girl's boyfriend stepped back, frightened. Suddenly, the girl spun in a circle and fell in a slumped position, growling and hissing. Bystanders who had gathered to watch threw down their drinks and cigarettes and asked the evangelists to pray for them. Suddenly, the girl's ponytail stood straight up and pumped up and down. Some of the people in the crowd screamed.

Moments later, a policeman tapped Janyce on the shoulder. "What's going on here?"

"This girl told us she wanted to be delivered from witchcraft." Janyce pointed at the girl slumped on the ground. "We prayed for her in the name of Jesus, and this happened."

The policeman looked at the girl. The girl fixed her eyes on the officer. "I'm not coming out of her. I'm going to kill her," screamed a shrill voice.

The policeman's eyes grew large. "Carry on!" he shouted to Janyce over his shoulder as he quickly walked down the street.

Janyce and her team prayed for the girl until she sat up and began praising God. Then the girl's boyfriend praised God, and the crowd that had gathered around them praised God. "It was exciting," said Janyce. "There is nothing boring about the power of God."

Janyce had worked with street people for several years when a desire entered her heart to move to the inner city. "I wasn't planning to start a rehab. I loved the street people and wanted to be near them. I was praying for a place to rent when a doctor gave me a triplex on First and Danneel," said Janyce. "The property sat in the middle of the St. Thomas, Magnolia, Melpomene, and Calliope housing projects. At the time, the neighborhood was so bad the police refused to go there alone. The triplex had no stove, hot water, or air conditioning. I cooked in Crock-Pots and electric skillets. In the summer, I draped wet towels over my body and let the fan blow on me. In the winter, I showered in cold water."

Janyce had been in the triplex for two weeks when gunshots, screaming, and sirens abruptly awoke her. She opened her front door. Four teenagers lay dead on the corner, a fifth boy badly wounded. She walked back into her house and found three-inch bullets on the floor and in her walls. Fear that she had missed the will of God gripped her. "I made a mistake," she prayed. "You couldn't have called me to a place this dangerous."

Janyce heard the Lord say, "Did you get shot?"

"No."

"Those who dwell in the secret place of the Most High shall abide under the shadow of the Almighty. I will protect you."

Janyce decided to stay and to fulfill her calling in the midst of a gang war that raged for weeks. She planned to start a church until malnourished, filthy, broken kids started knocking on her door. "Mama Janyce, you've got to help me," they pleaded.

"I couldn't turn them away, but I made it clear that they had to follow me as I followed Christ. If I prayed, they had to pray. If I studied the Bible, they had to study the Bible. If I distributed gospel tracts, they had to do it too. The next thing I knew, I was cooking for twenty people in Crock-Pots. They had to take cold showers too, but they had beds with clean sheets. Then the Lord told me to anoint my neighborhood with oil and pray."

Janyce walked the neighborhood, anointing everything with oil, but the bottle quickly ran dry. The next day, she carried a bucket of oil, which proved cumbersome. A friend saw her predicament and gave her a super-soaker that had a backpack. Janyce filled the backpack with oil and water, put on her multicolored straw hat, and walked to the corner where the young men had died.

Charles, a local gang leader, saw her. "Reverend, you got oil in that thing don't you?"

"Yeah, and it'll shoot fifty feet." She opened fire. Charles turned and fled.

A car pulled up with its passenger window down. The driver shouted, "Shoot him with the oil, Mama Janyce. He needs help." She aimed and fired. "Thank you," said the passenger as the car pulled away. Janyce walked the streets praying and anointing her neighborhood and nearby housing projects for many years.

One day, Janyce answered her door and was greeted by two men wearing suits who flashed their FBI badges. "Do you know anything about the Cotton Bomber?"

Janyce grinned and invited the agents inside. "I'm the Cotton Bomber."

"So you admit to bombing abortion clinics?"

"Spiritually, yes. We wrestle not with flesh and blood but with principalities, powers, and rulers of darkness."

"Do you want to explain that?" asked one of the agents.

"Some friends asked me to walk in a protest march in front of an abortion clinic, but I had a better plan. I told them to wait until night. We filled the super-soaker with oil so we didn't have to touch the building, which might set off an alarm. While we soaked the building down with oil, we bound the devils of Moloch (child sacrifice), Tamus (human sacrifice), and the spirits of Raman Habacathon (greed, murder, deception, lying, and fear). Then we buried cotton balls soaked in oil around the building as a barrier against evil spirits. I call it cotton bombing."

The agents looked at each other and then at Janyce. "Do you know anyone who would bomb an abortion clinic?"

"No. If I did, I'd tell you, because that is a sin."

The agent snapped his notepad shut and pocketed his pen. "Thank you for your time, ma'am."

If we believe the Bible, we cannot deny the existence of devils. Jesus encountered many. The devil tempted Jesus. Two demon-possessed men confronted Jesus. Devils screamed from human mouths, "You are the Son of God." Mary Magdalene had seven devils, and Jesus gave his disciples power to cast out devils. (Matthew 8:28, 10:8; Mark 3:15, 16:9; Luke 4:41)

While no one can prove Janyce's antics were effective in changing her neighborhood, no one can deny that the housing projects she anointed with oil and prayer have been torn down. Devils beware! Mama Janyce is looking for you. Her super-soaker is loaded, and she knows how to use it.

Who Is Anna Donahue?

I saw her for the first time as I walked by the TV carrying a basket of laundry. Just a glimpse—I didn't pay much attention. Matters of greater importance were on my mind: dirty underwear and mismatched socks. On the way to the grocery, I recognized the voice on the radio and turned up the volume. The woman I saw on TV had a name: Anna Donahue. Later that day, I surfed the Internet, and there she was again. Anna Donahue.

Anna's ministry website overflowed with activities: television and radio; annual daytime retreats for women; Mirror Mirror conferences for teenagers; Adopt-a-Widow Tea; Coming-Up-Higher Bible Studies. I wrote the date of the next Bible study on my calendar.

The cars parked on both sides of the street and the ones looking for a place to park, including mine, made the home that was hosting the study easy to find. I followed some women into the living room, which was already full, and considered myself fortunate to find an empty chair. As soon as I sat down, the woman next to me gushed with information about the profound effect of Anna's ministry on her life.

"Which one is Anna?" I inquired.

"She's not here yet," said the woman.

I turned my attention to the notes that had been thrust into my hand. The notes were neatly assembled in a three-prong folder, major points in bold print, each thought backed up with scripture, and a checklist at the end. Anna clearly invested her heart and soul into her teaching.

Suddenly, Anna burst into the room, charging the air with life, and greeted most of the women by name. The stranger among them—me—did not escape her attention. Her concern for everyone in the room was unmistakable. After the teaching, I handed her my business card and inquired if I could write a story about her ministry. Some might be suspicious of such an offer, but Anna received my inquiry with grace and humility.

Anna and I met for coffee several weeks later. She flooded me with questions, more concerned about who I was than talking about herself. After I satisfied all of her inquiries, it was my turn to ask questions.

Life couldn't have been better during Anna's sophomore year in college. One night she was watching television with friends when Gail walked into the community room. Anna saw a woman beaming like a light and heard muffled warnings.

"Gail's here!"

"Jesus freak."

"Wacko."

Gail's presence quickly cleared the room, leaving Anna and Gail alone. Anna had just met a young man and began a conversation with Gail about love and relationships. Gail looked at Anna and said, "The bottom line will be your relationship with Jesus Christ."

She wondered what Gail meant and rationalized that she knew God.

Gail had told Anna she needed to be born again to see the kingdom of God. Anna looked up the scripture in John chapter 3. She asked friends what it meant to be born again. They dismissed the subject as nonsense. Anna tried to dismiss Gail's warning by immersing herself in her journalism studies, but there was no escape.

Anna exited the college parking lot in her brown Dodge Dart, tears streaming down her face. What if Gail was right? What if there was more than being raised in a particular religion? She pulled her car to the side of the road and kneeled on the rough pavement. "Please," Anna prayed, "if you're real, I gotta know. I need help."

Suddenly, peace entered her heart and everything around her intensified. The grass looked greener, the sky bluer. She saw a bird in flight and was struck with the realization that God made the bird. "I can take you to the exact spot I had that experience," Anna assured me. "Months later my brother suggested I watch the 700 Club. Pat Robertson explained what it meant to be born again. I knelt by the TV and prayed for Jesus to come into my heart."

Anna graduated with a degree in broadcast journalism, married and moved to San Antonio, where she started her career making five dollars an hour as a rookie weekend reporter. When a plane crashed, the station sent her to obtain a comment from a family grieving the loss of their son. Anna objected to the intrusion into their grief. Her boss commanded her to go. She obeyed but knew this kind of broadcasting was not for her. As she endured the next year and a half to fulfill her contract, thoughts of Bible College entered her mind.

A job change for her husband sent them to New Orleans. They had already visited several churches when they walked into Victory Fellowship. Pastor Frank Bailey's sincerity and rich teaching convinced them to stay. Anna enrolled in the church's Bible College and looked for a place to serve. She hosted a short-lived television show sponsored by the church, taught Bible studies, and then became a section pastor in the women's ministry.

"As I worked in the church, I learned submission, how to yield to God's will, and how to discern his timing," said Anna. "The most important thing I learned was how to love people. I didn't care who they were, what they looked like, or how they smelled. I willingly embraced them. It was like having another born-again experience."

Anna had dreamed of leading her own ministry for many years. She was in a staff meeting when she knew the time had come. One of the leaders asked her about dates for upcoming events. She replied, "It's time for me to leave," and submitted her resignation. Instead of giving Anna a going-away party, the church held a baby shower to celebrate the birth of a new ministry: Anna Donahue's Ministry.

I couldn't understand why I had such a difficult time getting a good head shot of Anna to include with the article I wrote for NOLA's faith blog. Pictures abounded with her eyes closed, with her mouth open, with too much light, that were too dark, and with unflattering expressions she would not want public. I decided to ask Anna for a posed photo when I attended her Annual Daytime Women's Retreat. Ever gracious, she agreed to meet me outside so I could position her in a garden. Anna arrived with three friends. "Take a picture of all of us," said Anna. I complied. She let her friends step aside so I could take my photo, but I knew that I would not use it.

Paul wrote to the Philippians that some preach the gospel out of selfish ambition and some do so in love. As I spent time with Anna and those God gave her to shepherd, one thing shone brighter than the many facets of her ministry: the love between Anna and those who sit at her feet. I used the photo of Anna and the friends she loves.

Miracle at St. Rita's

The GPS squawked, "Take exit ramp to Lafayette Street." I whizzed past the exit.

"Recalculating," said the usually reliable voice in the little gray box.

"Go ahead and recalculate. I'm not going to Plaquemines Parish. I need directions to St. Bernard Parish," I grumbled. Forty minutes later, the box stopped recalculating in its quest to turn me around and announced, "Arriving at Jefferies." I looked right—a canal. I looked left—tall grass as far as the eye could see, not a building or warm body in sight. Ten minutes later, I passed hazardous material warnings, and the street dead-ended in front of a security shack.

I lowered the car window. The guard stuck her head inside. "You look familiar."

I ignored her comment and grinned to hide my frustration. "I don't want to go in the restricted area. Do you know where the House of Refuge is?"

"Nope, we're cleaning up the BP oil spill. No church here. Go back the way you came and take a right to get back on the highway."

I'd forgotten the backup map and phone numbers on my desk. Praying that my husband, who had worked the nightshift, would be awake, I called home. Rod stopped eating his Cheerios to rescue me. He called

Pastor Jefferies. Pastor Jefferies called me. Twenty minutes later, I pulled into the parking lot of House of Refuge to record a remarkable story.

"Throughout my teen years and into my adult life, I was depressed about life in general and constantly thought about suicide," began Pastor Jim Jefferies. Jim and his wife, Julie, were considering divorce when her brother witnessed to them about a loving God. Then Jim's father gave him a copy of *The Late Great Planet Earth* by Hal Lindsay. Jim accepted the book, thinking that it would bring some joy into his life. Instead, he read about the terrible judgments of God against sinful humanity. "Something about the book spoke to my heart, and I couldn't put it down," said Jim. "I decided if the things Lindsay wrote about were really going to happen, I owed it to myself to read the Bible."

Jim bought the biggest Bible he could find and started reading in the book of Genesis. Instead of finding a God of love, he saw a holy God who hated sin. Scriptures about a suffering Messiah encouraged Jim to continue reading as he searched for the God of love he had heard about.

He had just finished reading the book of Malachi when Julie's grandmother died. After the funeral, Julie remained with her family. Jim returned home, intent on reading Matthew, the first book in the New Testament. He turned to Matthew chapter 1 at midnight and read into the wee hours of the morning under the only light in his bedroom: a 100-watt lightbulb.

Jim read the last scripture in Matthew at 4:00 a.m. and closed his Bible. Jim knelt by his bedside and prayed, "I don't know who you are, but if you are real, please come into my heart and make yourself real to me."

"The moment I prayed, the room lit up like daytime. I cried like a baby as all that light and glory entered my heart. All of a sudden, I knew God loved me, and if I had been the only person on this planet needing salvation, he would have died for me. Tremendous joy flooded my heart."

The following Sunday Jim and Julie attended her brother's church and made a public confession of faith in Christ. "I didn't like people before I accepted Christ, but that changed. I became more open, bold," said Jim. "My classmates at the electrical school I attended saw the dramatic change, and I led some of them to the Lord."

Jim's pastor recognized the hand of God on Jim's life and invited him to teach a class for young married couples. "When I taught the class, I had understanding and messages that could have only come from God, so I asked the associate pastor how God calls people to ministry. The associate pastor replied, 'People who ask that question usually are.'" Jim pursued the educational requirements to become a minister. Shortly after he received a license to preach, he accepted the pastorate of Reggio Assembly of God.

"I told God, 'I quit,' at least once a week. The church was full of people who thought they should be the pastor. One man came early every Sunday morning and sat in my office with two ladies from the congregation. They wouldn't even get up when I walked in."

Jim decided he could throw the man out or ask God what to do. He opted for the less confrontational method. While Jim prayed for a solution, God told him to rearrange the furniture. He threw out an old bookcase and moved the desk to the other side of the office. Then he rearranged the chairs and other accessories the way he wanted them.

The following Sunday, the man was sitting in the sanctuary instead of the pastor's office. Shortly after that he announced that he was opening a church in his garage and asked for Jim's blessings. Most of the congregation left to attend the new church. Jim was glad the fighting had stopped but was depressed that his congregation had dwindled from fifty to fourteen members.

Jim knelt by his sofa and said, "Lord, I've had it."

He heard the Lord say, "You can leave if you want to."

"I can leave if I want to?"

"Yes," Jim heard the Lord say. "I never commanded you to go down there. I asked you to take that pastorate. You obeyed my voice, and I will bless you for it. I'll send you anywhere you want to go. It's your choice."

Jim considered God's offer and then replied, "I don't want another church. I'm going to stay here and do something for you."

God blessed Jim's small congregation, and its membership slowly increased. Jim formed a ministry team that visited St. Rita's Nursing Home every Wednesday and held services once a month. "We knew everyone in the nursing home by name, and we knew their families. I considered the residents as part of my congregation.

We loved them, ministered to them, hugged them, kissed them, and brought them Christmas gifts."

St. Rita's Nursing Home became the subject of national news when Sal and Mabel Mangano ignored a mandatory evacuation order as Hurricane Katrina roared toward the Louisiana coast. The Mangano's feared that evacuating would result in the death of several frail residents. The nursing home had been built on a patch of terra firma that did not flood during Hurricane Betsy in 1965. They believed they were safe.

The parking lot was dry and roof intact the morning of August 29, and the Manganos breathed a sigh of relief. Relief turned to horror when they heard a low rumbling sound and saw a wall of water rushing toward them. The water burst into the home and quickly rose to the ceiling, drowning thirty-five elderly residents.

Jim sat erect and grew animated. "I knew every resident who died at St. Rita's. We prayed with every one of them to receive Christ as their Savior long before a depression in the Gulf turned into a killer hurricane."

Everyone knew about the tragedy at St. Rita's Nursing Home. It's the kind of story that makes people sneer, "Where was God?" I doubt anyone except Jim knew how God honored his decision to remain in a difficult pastorate and "do something for God." He became the messenger God used to save the eternal souls of those who drowned.

Thank You

My attendance at a writing critique group unexpectedly ended. I awoke the next morning, perplexed. I had attended the group for years and didn't want to leave, but I knew that it was time to move on. On the heels of leaving the group, a name kept coming to my attention: Linda Rodriguez.

Linda led a Christian writers group. We connected via Facebook. Her writing group had not been meeting, but she wanted to start again. She revived The Holy Scriptors long enough for me to meet her husband, Pastor David Rodriguez. Before the group disbanded again, I asked David if I could write his profile for NOLA's faith blog.

I tried to find a mutually agreeable date to meet with Linda and David without success. Linda is a gifted writer, so I asked her to write the article. She consented, and that was the last I heard from her until someone called my name as I walked out of a restaurant. I turned around to see Linda's smiling face. She had been busy and didn't think she would have time to write the article.

I asked Pastor David, seated beside her, if he still wanted an article written. He did. I made an appointment to meet at his church office. I didn't need directions to Christian Fellowship Church. I had attended the church on 5049 Ehret Road when I was a teenager, and it was called Marrero Assembly of God. Shortly before and during the two years I attended Marrero Assembly of God, I had spiritual experiences that are as vivid today as they were in 1973. The church holds a significant place in my heart.

David led me to a room he uses for counseling, and we sat at opposite ends of a long table. For the first time since I started writing about local Christians, I would record a story without coffee machines grinding, music blasting, and the neighboring table's conversation in the background. But a greater gift than that awaited. Before our conversation ended, David solved a thirty-eight-year-old mystery.

David encountered God in an old-fashioned tent revival, complete with sawdust on the ground. The evangelist brought his fiery message to a close and pleaded for willing hearts to come to the altar.

David looked at his friend seated next to him. "Do you want to go?"

"Do you?" his friend replied.

"I'll go if you go."

The boys slipped out of their seats and walked the sawdust trail to the altar. The next thing David remembered was lying flat on his back with a feeling of refreshing flowing over him and a foreign language coming from his mouth, which Pentecostals call "tongues."

"That experience marked my life," said David. "From that point on, I knew with certainty that I was God's child. Then I became a teenager, and the hormones from hell kicked in. When I was fourteen, I decided being a Christian was too hard. I knew I would die and go to hell if I turned away from God, but I figured I'd have a lot of fun before I got there."

Four years later, David's fun came to an abrupt end when he stole a car with a friend and found himself staring through the bars of a Georgia jail. The small cell aggravated his claustrophobia, magnifying his suffering. He paced the cell, longing to be free, and then he remembered the prayer of Cain and pleaded for mercy. "Lord, my punishment is greater than I can bear" (Genesis 4:13).

The next day, David called home and told his father what happened. His father replied with calm assurance, "David, the Lord spoke to me. You're coming home tomorrow."

"But Dad," David objected, "I'm five hundred miles from home, and I don't have money to hire an attorney." His father stood steadfast on God's promise. David hung up the phone and was escorted to his cell with little hope of being released. The next day, his friend's father posted bail for both of them, and the judge ordered them to return in August for sentencing.

David returned to New Orleans and met a girl who introduced him to marijuana. He was experimenting with hallucinogenic drugs when he stood before a Georgia judge for sentencing. David knew God had heard his prayer for mercy when the judge gave them probation instead of a jail sentence, but his gratitude for a lighter punishment was short lived.

The guilt of spurning God's mercy weighed heavily on David. When he partied with his friends, conviction gripped him. While his friends enjoyed the hallucinations, David often spoiled the party by announcing they were all going to hell and preaching to them. When his girlfriend became pregnant, he married her, but the marriage quickly fell apart. His wife left him and then learned she was pregnant with David's second son. David lay on his bed and cried out in despair, "God, why is this happening to me?"

He reached for the Bible lying beside him and flipped it open. Proverbs chapter 6 glared at him: "A scoundrel and villain, who goes about with a corrupt mouth, who winks with his eye, signals with his feet and motions with his fingers, who plots evil with deceit in his heart—he always stirs up dissension. Therefore disaster will overtake him in an instant; he will suddenly be destroyed—without remedy" (Proverbs 6:12-15).

"I felt I was reading my life story and God was showing me why he was about to throw me into hell" said David. "I remember dropping on my knees, shaking with fear, and saying, 'God, I am sorry,' but I didn't ask God to forgive me. I chose hell when I was fourteen and thought it was too late. When I stood, I felt a hot pressure and heard a mocking echo in my mind: 'It's too late. It's too late.'"

That evening, David's father visited him. During the course of their conversation, his father said, "The devil will tell you that you are going crazy." When David heard those words, the oppression choking him with despair lifted.

David smiled. "It's easier to appreciate God's grace when you have tasted his justice. I tell people I got saved in 1970, but that's not entirely accurate. That afternoon, reading Proverbs, I knew I had crossed the line with God, but he spared me. Instead of giving me the hell I chose, he restored me."

David reconnected with Jeb, a high school friend who had also committed his life to Christ. On weekends, David and Jeb returned to their old haunt, a local Dairy Queen, and told anyone who would listen that they had found something better than drugs. Jeb's car was often packed to capacity with teenagers desiring to learn more about Jesus the following Sunday. When David wasn't sharing his faith in Christ, he worked as an assistant manager for Shakey's Pizza Parlor and fought for custody of his two children.

Several months after David's restoration, a woman approached him with a prophecy that she believed was for him. She had felt the unction to speak it during the service, but being a new Christian, she was reluctant to prophesy publically. She told David, "Thus says the Lord, 'My son, when I set you free, you are free indeed. I have a work for you that you know nothing of.'"

Shortly after the prophecy, an opportunity for David to become general manager of a Shakey's Pizza Parlor arose, but David had a dilemma. To become general manager of his own store, he had to reveal that he had a felony conviction. The general manager knew David was on probation, but the owner of the Louisiana franchise did not. David told his probation officer about his predicament. His probation officer called the franchise owner to express the dramatic and positive changes he had seen in David since he was placed on probation.

"The next thing I know, I received a letter from the Atlanta judge complimenting me on how well I have handled myself since the conviction. He had terminated my probation and ordered that my judgment be set aside. My record was cleared, as though it never happened. Then my former wife, who was still on drugs, decided our boys would be better off with me and gave me custody. I rented an apartment in New Orleans East, picked up my sons on Valentine's Day 1971, and started my job as a general manager of my own store the next day. It was like the hand of God wiped everything clean. Then in the spring of 1972, Jeb told me he was starting a ministry called The House of Living Water, and he wanted me to run it."

At this point in David's story, I heard him talking, but I wasn't listening. My mind was flooded with memories. God had revealed himself to me at The House of Living Water in August 1973. I wondered if David was talking about the same place and struggled to concentrate as he continued his story.

"Jeb and another man planned to fix up a building in old Algiers. I would live at The House of Living Water and run the ministry while they went to Bible college. I was in walking distance from the Shakey's I managed in New Orleans East. Moving to the west bank meant a twenty-six-mile round trip, but I accepted the position and moved into the building with my sons."

"What year was this?" I asked.

"1972," he repeated.

The year didn't fit my experience, but the location did. The place I had encountered the living God was on Opelousas Street in old Algiers. I remembered two things about the preacher whose message led me to accept Christ: he was young and had a beard. I studied David's face, trying to imagine how he would look with a beard, and listened intently as he continued his story.

"The manager of the Shakey's on Veterans resigned. I was managing the smallest restaurant in the chain and next in line for the bigger store. The Veteran's Shakey's was in disrepair, and I felt like I could grow in New Orleans East. I had already made up my mind to turn it down when the owner of the chain came to talk to me. The owner said, 'The manager of the Veteran's store has left, and I want you to take over the Gretna Shakey's.' He was an older man. I thought he had a senior moment, so I corrected him. 'You mean the Veteran Shakey's.' Then he corrected me. 'No, the manager of the Gretna Shakey's has seniority over you. He wants the Veteran Shakey's.' The Gretna Shakey's was the plum in the chain, the biggest and nicest of all the stores and located minutes away from The House of Living Water. God worked everything out, and I stayed at The House of Living Water until late in 1973—"

"I was saved at The House of Living Water in August 1973," I exclaimed. "I never knew the preacher's name, but I remember he was young and had a beard."

"I had a beard," said David.

David had more than a beard. He kept a small photo album in his office with pictures from that time in his life. I looked at a picture yellowed with age of a young David with a beard and said, "It was you!"

It's never too late to say thank you, and I thanked David for his obedience to God that led me to salvation.

What are the odds that the man God used to lead me to Christ would now pastor the first church I attended after my salvation—the same church where God unfolded and confirmed his plan for my life? What are the odds that I would return to 5049 Ehret Road thirty-eight years later and learn the identity of "the young preacher with a beard"? The odds are slim, but God's kindness is great. I walked out of Christian Fellowship knowing God had used me to comfort, encourage, and assure a faithful servant that his labor in the Lord is not in vain.

Teena Myers

Friends

Rod and I were on the way to the grocery store. I looked up from playing with my phone—I wasn't driving—and read "Anthony Marquize for U.S. Congress District 2" on a billboard. My attention quickly returned to the phone.

We loaded our groceries into the car and took a different route home. Young adults were standing by the road side waving signs—Anthony Marquize for U.S. Congress District 2. "Look, Rod. I saw a billboard with that name on the way to the grocery." Too late. We were past the sign wavers before I finished my statement.

The milk was in the fridge, cereal in the cabinet, and I was seated comfortably in my recliner watching TV when the doorbell rang. My husband answered. Groan. Whatever they are selling, he's gonna buy it! He stepped outside and shut the door. Ten minutes later, Rod handed me a business card, Anthony Marquize for U.S. Congress District 2.

"What is this, Anthony Marquize day?" I flipped Anthony's card over and read "For he is the minister of God to thee for good" (Romans 13:4, KJV). I entertained the thought of contacting Mr. Marquize for less than five seconds. I already had ten people waiting for me to write an article about their ministries. I didn't need to add another to the list.

A few days later, I attended a minister's fellowship meeting. Need I tell you who was present? Anthony

Marquize was running for the House of Representatives in Louisiana's 2nd District as an Independent against Anh Joseph Cao, the first Vietnamese American elected to the United States Congress, and Obama-backed Cedric Richmond. Need I tell you what I did?

Anthony was sitting on his sofa watching Fox News and complaining about the state of government. Glenn Beck addressed the warning in Ezekiel chapter 33. If the watchman doesn't warn people when he sees trouble coming and they perish, God will hold the watchman accountable for their blood. Then Beck raised his hands and said, "Blood will not be on my hands, because I'm warning the people."

"At that moment, I felt like the Lord said to me 'Anthony, stop complaining or get up and do something.' I stood and said to my wife, 'Jeannette, I'm running for Congress.' When I stood, something happened inside me that gave me the resolve to run this race."

Anthony married Jeannette when he was nineteen. That year his father suffered a heart attack. Running the family business became Anthony's responsibility. "When my wife and I had our first child, our marriage was turbulent. I thought Jeannette should be happy with the things I provided. When she wasn't, I blamed her for all my problems."

Anthony tried drinking to escape the pressures of life. Alcohol made him sick, so he turned to drugs. Getting high on weekends soon became a daily affair. Meanwhile, Jeannette's unhappiness increased. One day she cried to God, "I don't believe anyone loves me. If you don't help me, in three days I'm going to kill myself."

Three days later, Anthony answered a knock at their door. The man holding a Bible said, "I'm Pastor Savage from the Baptist Mission. I'd like to tell you about Jesus. Can I come in?"

"In my mind I said, 'No, I'm Catholic,' but that's not what came out of my mouth. He was the most knowledgeable man I've ever met. I asked him hundreds of questions about Jesus and the Bible. He answered every one with a scripture."

The Marquizes attended the pastor's church the following Sunday. Jeannette accepted Christ, but the radical transformation in her life troubled Anthony. "In the past, I blamed her unhappiness for all my problems. Now that she was happy, I couldn't blame her anymore. I knew what she felt was real, and I knew that I didn't have it."

Anthony stopped attending church when he opened a seafood restaurant. He spent his days at the family business and his nights at the restaurant. His marriage was at the point of divorce when he encountered God while driving sixty miles per hour down the interstate.

Anthony was listening to the book of Matthew on tape when the narrator said, "How can you say to your brother, Let me take the speck out of your eye, when all the time there is a plank in your own eye? You hypocrite, first take the plank out of your own eye, and then you will see clearly to remove the speck from your brother's eye" (Matthew 7:4-5). At that point, Anthony realized that he could not blame his wife for all his problems. "I said to God, 'I'm wrong.' The moment I said that, the power of God came into my truck and set me free. I don't know how to explain what happened next. I raised both hands and praised God. Fifteen minutes later, I put my hands back on the steering wheel. My truck was still going sixty miles per hour on the interstate. As soon as I touched the steering wheel, I heard God's voice."

God said to Anthony, "I will give you a high so much greater than drugs, you will never want them again." Anthony rolled down the window of his truck and threw out more than a thousand dollars' worth of drugs. Then he reached for a cigarette and heard, "You don't need anything but me." Anthony threw his cigarettes out the window, and then he heard God say, "I hate divorce."

"We've hurt each other so much we don't even like each other," said Anthony. "But I'll go back home if you will love my wife through me." Anthony returned home and felt a supernatural strength to love his wife that healed their marriage.

Anthony served as an elder at his church for six years before accepting the pastorate at a church in Venice, Louisiana. Under his leadership, the congregation grew from five to three hundred. Ten years later, God sent him to Russia, where he lived for three years. During that time he planted twenty churches and cofounded the Global Strategy Christian Association Evangelical Faith. Anthony continues to oversee the association which has grown to sixty-two churches.

"If I hadn't lived in Russia, I don't think I would have run for Congress," said Anthony. "Our government is trying to implement the same kind of socialist ideas that are in Russia. I've seen firsthand the result of a centralized government that controls everything a country produces. Moscow is well maintained, but the rest of the country is one large ghetto. Most of the places we stayed didn't have running water. The apartments were dilapidated, even the concrete stairs were falling apart. The streets were horrible, but it didn't matter in some respects because very few people could afford a car. All the stores were government owned. You had to go to a bakery to buy bread, go to another store for meat, yet another store for vegetables, and there were long lines at all of the stores. It took all day to buy a few items from the sparsely stocked shelves. Standing in a crowd was eerily quiet. No one spoke because the people feared what the government might do to them if they complained."

Anthony ran an ambitions campaign for Congress, hoping to make a difference. He lost the seat to liberal Democrat Cedric Richmond but left us with something far greater. In Richmond's victory speech, he said, "Pastor Anthony Marquize ran a great race. He is going to be a very valuable asset to this community, and he is a dear friend of mine now. As we got to know one another, we decided that there are more things we have in common than things that separate us."

Anthony failed to obtain a seat of power in government. His supporters were disappointed. I wasn't. God gave us something greater in Anthony: a shining light that people with different ideologies can be friends who work together for the good of all.

The Communications Guy

I had heard about the Greater New Orleans Pastor's Coalition (GNOPC) but knew little more than the coalition existed. When Rev. Eskine sent me an e-mail about the coalition's upcoming activities, I visited its website. A dark-red italicized phrase caught my eye: "We are always looking to include other pastors and churches. For more information, contact Paul Malinich." I sent an e-mail to Paul suggesting that a story about the coalition on NOLA's faith blog might encourage greater involvement.

I sipped a vanilla iced coffee and Paul a large Diet Coke while we discussed the formation of the GNOPC and how Paul—who is not a pastor—became part of a pastor's coalition. His attitude of service was immediately evident. "I'm not the leader of the coalition," said Paul. "I will stay to serve the pastors until I'm no longer needed."

Several days after chatting with Paul, I attended a ministers meeting, and his name surfaced as one of the "leaders" of the coalition, a title I surmised Paul would quickly deny. He already informed me that he was the "communications guy" who had obtained permission from the pastors to meet with me.

Finding Faith in the City Care Forgot

"In 1999, my life went through a season of purging," said Paul. "Everything disagreeable to God fell by the wayside, even some things I didn't think were all that bad. The following year I attended a Promise Keepers conference hoping to connect with other Christian men."

The Promise Keepers 2000 theme "Go the Distance," based on Hebrews 12:1, set the stage for Paul to run his race with perseverance. He returned from the conference with renewed zeal and looked forward to World Communion Sunday. Paul loved the annual United Methodist Church service that encouraged Christians to connect with one another to achieve a common goal.

"The day of the service, I awoke angry," said Paul, "but I didn't go to bed angry. I had been distressed with the lack of unity in the church for a long time. That morning, my distress changed to righteous anger and I felt a strong urge to fast and pray."

Paul embarked on a twenty-one-day water fast. Since he loved junk food, his last two meals before the fast were cookies and caramel corn. He suffered physically as the water he drank cleansed toxins from his body. His legs were numb for days. Sores erupted on his back. By the nineteenth day of the fast, Paul realized he had stopped praying according to his own wisdom. On the last day of the fast, he received a vision of his future ministry.

Paul and a group of friends who shared his passion established Set Free Ministries outside the auspices of the Methodist Church. "We decided God is too big to be confined to one church." Paul forsook a profitable career in accounting and sold all his worldly possessions. Working as a missionary for Set Free Ministries, he moved annually to assist churches in the development of administration, discipleship, and outreach. The annual relocation of his family stopped when God led him to a city cleansed by water.

A year after Hurricane Katrina devastated the Gulf Coast, Paul came to New Orleans through Billy Graham's chaplaincy program. He stayed three months and returned for several ten-day visits. His family became permanent residents when he met Dennis Watson, the pastor of Celebration Church. Pastor Watson offered Paul and his family lodging in a trailer on the church's campus.

The Greater New Orleans Pastor's Coalition started before Paul arrived. Shortly after the hurricane, area pastors realized the need created by the disaster was more than one church could meet. After decades of isolation, area pastors called one another to exchange supplies, share resources, and organize the steady flow of volunteers coming to New Orleans.

Pastor Watson ran an advertisement inviting churches to work together. The first meeting drew 120 pastors. Pastor Watson challenged the pastors to walk the path of humility so they could unite and work as God's agents to heal a wounded city. The pastors rose to the challenge. Seven years after a disaster drew them together, they still meet to encourage, strengthen, and help one another.

By the time Paul arrived in New Orleans, the focus of his ministry had moved from helping individual churches flourish to a broader mission of helping the church as a whole work toward a common goal. His new focus found its fulfillment in serving pastors struggling to rebuild their devastated city. Paul's training in business administration made him the perfect candidate to become the "communications guy." He keeps the pastors informed of the coalition's activities and assists wherever he is needed.

The tragedy created by Hurricane Katrina bound pastors in New Orleans together in a spirit of unity. Together they have achieved more than they could have done alone. That a man cleansed by water found his destiny in a city cleansed by water did not escape my attention. Paul is God's gift of love to pastors struggling under a weight too heavy for one shepherd to carry alone.

Atheist Said

I've had the pleasure of hearing many compelling stories that reaffirmed my faith in a living God, but no one strengthened my conviction of the truth in the gospel more than David Brown. I met David while attending a secular writer's critique group. The first time he critiqued one of my distinctly Christian submissions, he declared, "I don't believe any of this. I'm an atheist."

"I'm not here to argue theology," I assured David. "Comments on my material are limited to the mechanics of writing." Satisfied that he had not walked into an evangelistic trap, he consistently gave me critiques that brought clarity to my writing. During one of the meetings, he told the group about constructing Aaron's gold cow. I was intrigued that an atheist would build an image of a deity and asked David if I could write about his experience. He consented to meet me at a local bookstore.

David sat down at the small, round table, clutching a cup of Starbucks coffee, to tell me how Christian zealots provoked him to bring a gold cow to Mardi Gras. Our conversation unexpectedly drifted into matters of faith. I left my recorder on, thinking the exchange would be brief. It wasn't.

"I discovered there is no Santa Claus when I was seven," said David, "and it taught me an important lesson: everyone around you can tell you something exists, and it really doesn't. One day I was sitting on a swing, thinking about that and about my neighbor's claim that angels watch over us. I thought, *Yeah, right.* It sounded like so much nonsense to me. I told my mother I don't believe there is a God. She told me religion and faith had been a comfort, something she really did not want to let go of, but she agreed with me. My mother had some bad experiences with priests, and I think my comment helped her sever the cord with religion."

"There have been times I wanted to wash my hands of the church, but I've always gone back. It's not fair to blame God for everything people do in his name," I replied.

David spoke with calm conviction. "If you treat people with respect, I don't care what your core beliefs are. What a person believes does not define them. We can have the same core beliefs yet treat people entirely different. Our actions define us."

"I agree with you."

"I firmly believe the head should rule the heart," David continued. "Gut instincts should not be the deciding factor. But there is a spiritual side to human beings. Everyone seeks this deeper emotional satisfaction, a moment when you feel connected to things outside yourself, whether it is the universe or God or whatever you want to call it. You can get that a lot of places not just in church.

"My uncle found his experience outside the church. He always found a reason to be out hunting or whatever on Sunday. One day, my Mom asked him why he didn't want to go to church. He took her to a clearing in the woods with tall trees all around and sunlight slanting through the branches and said, 'This is my church.' He understood his spiritual side."

I pondered David's comments while I sipped my coffee and then replied, "David, where did you get the idea that faith has no reason and Christians blindly believe without rational thought? There is a verse in Romans chapter ten that says faith comes by hearing and hearing by the word of God. Christians interpret that verse to mean hearing the word preached or reading the Bible imparts faith, but that's not true. Paul identified the word of God by quoting from Psalm nineteen, which says 'The heavens declare the glory of God; the skies proclaim the work of his hands. Day after day they pour forth speech; night after night they display knowledge. There is no speech or language where their voice is not heard. Their voice goes out into all the earth, their words to the ends of the world.' The things God created without human speech are more reliable and speak louder than a multitude of words from one of God's people because they are the voice of his actions."

"Teena, there are two ways to determine truth: revelation or reason—in layman's terms, the heart or the head. Your heart can lead you astray, so you really need to use your head or reason. Deductive reasoning says things have happened this way in the past, and that teaches me what is going to happen in the future, but that is not necessarily true. I believe in inductive reasoning. Look at the facts and then try to make a reasonable decision.

"Theology is philosophy as applied to faith, and the theologian will always have a faith element. Some completely reject reason as Martin Luther, who said, 'To be a Christian you must pluck out the eye of reason.' On the other hand, Thomas Aquinas tried to use Aristotelian logic to prove God exists and the dogmas of the Catholic Church were accurate. From my perspective, there is a sort of bastardization from Christians who follow the rationalist viewpoint. For all their love of reason, when you get to the very core of their beliefs, it all comes back to the revealed word as the source upon which they build reason.

"To persuade me God exists, you have to convince me truth lies in listening to the little voice in my heart rather than looking at the world around me, and I'm just not going to believe that. To persuade you God doesn't exist, I have to convince you that the little voice inside you lies and is not the most accurate thing for you to be paying attention to."

At this point in our conversation, I found David's reasoning flawed. He does not have to convince me the little voice in my heart is unreliable. The Bible warns us "The heart is deceitful above all things, and desperately wicked..." (Jeremiah 17:9). Therefore, I would never tell David to listen to the little voice in his heart rather than look at the world around him.

I also agree with David's assessment that our beliefs do not define us. Martin Luther's beliefs do not define me, nor does Luther define God. God's actions define him, so why did David turn a deaf ear to the voice his uncle heard, the voice of God's actions? We can look at the world around us and come to some reasonable conclusions that are not based on a little voice within or a book but on evidence that is seen, touched, and felt.

It is reasonable to conclude that a power greater than man exists because there are many things in this world that exceed human ability. We are dependent on sunlight to survive, but we do not control when the sun rises or sets. We are dependent on rain but cannot control when, where, and how much rain will fall. We cannot stop a hurricane, harness the power in a tornado, nor calm an earthquake.

There is a vast universe of planets and stars. Man has traveled no farther than the moon and never reached the deepest depths of the ocean floor. From where did all I can see that is so much greater and stronger than man is originate if there is no power greater than man? An even greater puzzle is why forces we cannot control work together to sustain human life.

Life abounds from the whale that dwarfs man in size to cells so tiny human eyes need aide to observe their behavior, yet man has not created one living being. Did man decide if we would have two legs or four? Did man put flight in the wings of a bird or give fish the ability to breathe under water? Did we give ourselves the ability to speak, to think, or to reason?

I can attain a reasonable conclusion that the resurrection of the human body, a major foundation of Christian faith, is possible by looking at the world around me. In fact, I only need to consider a seed, which I can touch, see, and witness its ability to transform. An apple seed, so small it fits in the palm of my hand, when planted in the ground, dies. If conditions are right, enough sunlight and rain, something completely different from the seed will sprout from the ground: a tree. In time, the tree will produce apples, and within the apples will be seeds. The seed I planted in the ground did not cease to exist; it only multiplied and returned greater than it was before it died. Therefore, based on what I observe in the world around me, why should I believe that I will simply cease to exist when I die? I also began as one cell, one seed in my mother's womb.

David addressed me as though he already knew what I thought and already understood how I came to embrace faith. I have not relied on a little voice within but looked at the world around me and made reasonable conclusions based on observable facts.

David paused to check his cell phone and then addressed his distaste for evangelism. "Problems arise when people aggressively try to convert a person to a different point of view. That doesn't mean that the little voice inside you is not important. This is where I have conflict with some atheists. You have to feed that part of yourself. If you have to create transcendent experiences by standing on the edge of the Grand Canyon to feel the wonder of it, then you should. If music transports you, spend every weekend at the opera. Do whatever you need to do. Am I making sense?"

"There is a lot you say that makes sense, David, except your conviction that faith has no reason and all Christians base their faith on a feeling."

"It's all based on Scripture, isn't it?"

"There are two covenants recorded in the Bible, David. A covenant of grace made with Abraham based on faith God would keep his word. God repeated that covenant to Isaac and Jacob, but Jacob wanted to wheel and deal with God. He wanted a binding agreement, which put stipulations upon both parties. If God added the provision of food and clothes to his promise, Jacob vowed to tithe and build a church. When he reneged on his vow, Jacob's life fell apart and God sent Jacob back to Bethel to keep his vow.

"Jacob's children knew the consequences of failing to keep an agreement. Yet they willingly, with full understanding of the consequences, agreed to a covenant of law that blessed you if you obeyed and cursed you if you didn't. Israel reneged on its deal with God too. Before God allowed the full force of the curse in the law to come upon their nation, he sent Jesus to call them back to the faith of Abraham—a faith that works when we love God and one another."

David leaned forward; his eyes studied me intently. "That is the first time you used the word *love*."

"You can't stop at the covenant of law and understand God. That covenant is temporary."

"In that case, why is anything in the Old Testament relevant if there is a completely new covenant?"

"To teach us the fallacy of dealing with God on any basis but love—"

"I don't see a lot of love from God in the Old Testament." David's words dripped with sarcasm. "I have a problem with the character of God as presented in the Old Testament. I have a superior set of ethics. I really do. If I honestly believed that the God of the Old Testament is the God in charge of everything, I would have to make myself his implacable foe because he is not a nice guy."

"If God's only attribute is law, I would have to agree, but—"

"But then along comes the New Testament thing."

"The New Testament explains the depth of God's love."

"But doesn't the Bible say God hardened the heart of Pharaoh? Where is the love in that?"

"The Hebrew word translated, *harden* means 'to heal, to cure, to repair.' God repeatedly tried to heal Pharaoh's heart by giving him observable, verifiable facts a living God had requested religious freedom for his people. Moses told Pharaoh what God would do, God did it, and then Pharaoh checked to see if it really happened. Pharaoh knew the truth. Not once but twice he said to Moses, 'I have sinned. The Lord is righteous.' Yet he stubbornly refused to let Israel worship their God."

"Now we are getting into real rationalist issues," said David. "The interpretation of Hebrew is hotly debated among people who spend their entire lives translating Hebrew. I watched a special on the Dead Sea Scrolls, and an argument erupted between Jewish, Christian, and Muslim scholars. They each had a different interpretation of the same passage of scripture. I thought they would come to blows over what a few passages mean. How can I be sure any of them are right about what a word means?"

"By listening to the voice your uncle listened to—"

"There you go. We're back to that little voice that gives revelation. That is what I said before. In its core, faith always comes down to a personal revelation. When you really get all the way back to the very first reason you walked down this path, like you said, you got to listen to that little voice."

"No, David, you are putting words in my mouth that I did not say. I'm not talking about a little voice in me. I'm talking about the voice of God's actions—a voice you already acknowledged is reliable when you said our actions define us. Nature speaks in a language everyone can understand. To me, truth is found in the justice of God's actions. If it's not based on justice, if it's not right, and if it's not right for everyone, past, present and future, it's not truth."

David looked thoughtful. "Well…I will agree with you. I suppose from a Christian perspective, my great sin is pride. I honestly believe that I know what is right and wrong. I really do."

"David, I absolutely agree with you. After Adam and Eve sinned, God said, 'The man has now become like one of us, knowing good and evil.' That knowledge is innate in us. We call it 'conscience.'"

"This is one thing on which you and atheists agree," said David.

"I think you are a lot closer to God than you think, but there are things about God that you don't understand.

"When I think about it metaphorically, yes, I would agree with you. A friend told me everything in the Old Testament refers to the coming of Jesus. But I just can't buy that. When I read the Bible, it's obvious flawed people wrote it. One example is the story of the gold calf. The priest in the temple of Jerusalem really didn't like the competition that Jeroboam's worship places provided. The gold calf worship sucked revenues away from Jerusalem, so they included the story about the gold calf being evil to discourage people from shopping in someone else's store."

"David, do you know why the gold calf was considered evil?"

"I understand theologically why. It's idolatry, 'thou shalt not worship images.' They were specifically violating the word of God."

"They were doing more than that. They were violating love."

David looked puzzled. "You are violating love by worshiping a gold image?"

"Yes, David. God promised to be one hundred percent devoted to Israel and never fail them. All he asked in return was for them to be one hundred percent devoted to him. All the other sins they committed could be atoned for. When they constructed the gold calf and bowed before it, they spit in God's face considering the price he had to pay for their deliverance."

"I think the Ten Commandments and the story of the gold calf were added afterward. It reads like an afterthought. The story is sort of an appendix. Especially when I learned there were gold calves in the northern part of the country that people worshiped. It just seems to fit in, to me.

"If you are a member of the priesthood and you are transcribing the holy text, it doesn't hurt to throw in something about how God doesn't want you to shop at the competition's store. That is just the way it reads to me."

"The same applies to connecting the Old Testament to the New Testament. It seems absurd to me. They seem completely separated. The Old Testament is a bundle of cultural stories and myths about Israel. The New Testament is about one person within a culture who provided a revolt and a revival of the culture at the same time."

"If you understood the law God gave to Moses, you would understand why Christians say that. Jesus's life was a fulfillment of the law. Moses told them a prophet would come with a ministry similar to his. The nation was waiting for that prophet's arrival when Jesus was born."

"I understand that, it all comes down to this. I just don't buy the premise," said David.

David said, "I just don't buy that," "It seemed to fit," "seems absurd to me," "just seems irrational to me," "I just don't buy the premise." I couldn't help but wonder if David was listening to the voice he told me is corrupt and can't be trusted. If he had given me facts to substantiate his feelings, I might have a reason to seriously consider his objections.

David stated that the translation of scripture is not reliable. Yet he is sure God is "not a nice guy" based on scripture. Would a person with a superior set of ethics make judgments about someone he or she has never met based on the things flawed people wrote or translated? If we cannot trust the translation of the Hebrew language, David has no reasonable basis to believe God hardened Pharaoh's heart to destroy him.

In the Exodus story, Pharaoh acknowledged his sin. David almost did the same when he said, "I suppose, from a Christian perspective, my great sin is pride."

"David, it's your position that the Bible cannot be trusted because it was written and translated by man, but every book in this bookstore was written by man. Based on your argument, we can't believe anything in any of these books."

"In many of these books, there are false statements mixed with truth. I will not say the Bible is full of falsehoods. There is a certain amount of historical fact in the Bible, be it however corrupt and disguised. The entire Bible shouldn't be tossed out, but I will say it does not contain any more truth than other books," said David.

"The Bible teaches us a specific truth. The truth about God and what it means to love," I replied.

"I don't think any road you take is a sure path to making better people. To me, being a better person is what life is all about. I'm on the same side as anybody who is looking for justice and wants people to treat each other well in this world. I'm with anyone who wants to end mindless violence so we can live together in peace. To me, it is irrelevant what the philosophical basis of that person's desire is. The important thing is the goal and those basic values. Would you agree with me?"

"Yes. I've had opportunity to talk to people of different faiths. We all want the same things, but we have different concepts about God that divides us."

"Think of it this way, Teena. You reach a point in your life when you continue to have all the beliefs that you have but your focus moves away from religion. You continue to treat people around you decently and try hard to be a good person. As long as you are taking care of the nuts and bolts, doesn't the spiritually take care of itself? I mean, the reason you are very interested in this sort of thing, isn't it more that you personally find it very interesting than that it is really necessary for salvation?"

"Being a good person won't save me from death, David."

"True."

"If there is nothing else, if this life is all there is, I've been cheated. Why should I be a stepping stone to a better future that I will never have a part in? There is no justice in that."

"But if you are focusing on your family and the people around you and being a good person, would you consider that to be as valid a form of serving God as studying the Bible and getting involved in theology?"

"It's not about theology, David. It's about love. My husband loves me more than most but not like God does. I've never met anyone who hasn't lied to me, and I've told a few lies myself. I've never met anyone who has believed the best of me, even when I have acted my worst. I've never met anyone who would continue to believe in me when no one else would. I have found that experience in God."

"I agree that people will always let you down. We need a reason to keep living. Why do we continue to struggle? We need to find something that is a rock, something we will always be able to rely on."

Talking to my atheist friend confirmed the veracity of the Bible and strengthened my faith. He knows we need a rock yet rejects the rock God gave us in Jesus. I listened intently as David explained the rock he relies on to make life worth living.

"I had an epiphany when I visited an exhibition of impressionist paintings at the National Gallery of Art in Washington DC. I had only seen reproductions of these paintings. In person, they were overwhelming. The paint seemed to have light sources behind it. For me, it was a religious experience. I walked out of the gallery stunned and thought about the things that have always given me pleasure. Reliable things, like great movies that I can watch over and over, books that give me satisfaction every time I read them. Music is never going to let me down. The things people create, products of the human mind, they are my rock."

David's rock drew a sharp contrast between the Atheist and Christian. The Atheist worships that which flawed humans create. The Christian worships the one who gave humanity the ability to create. David refuses to believe in God because he questions God's ethics yet found a reason to live in the creations of unethical people.

"My problem with philosophers and theologians is this," said David. "Reality, goodness, and justice are more visceral and concrete than a system of thought or religious doctrine. There is a wonderful movie called *Hotel Terminus* by Marcel Ophuls about Klaus Barbie, the 'Butcher of Lyon.' One woman Ophuls interviewed tells how two Gestapo agents came to her apartment on the fifth floor and arrested her and her family. As they were going down the stairs, they paused on a landing. Her neighbor, I think her name was Mrs. Bauteaux, opened her door a crack to see what was happening. When the neighbor saw the Gestapo were distracted, she reached out her hand to pull a six-year-old girl into her apartment. She almost had her in the apartment when one of the Gestapo agents saw her. He shoved the apartment door open, smacked the woman, and took the little girl. The woman said she would always remember Mrs. Bauteaux, who, at tremendous risk to her life, tried to save the little girl. At the end of the film, Ophuls dedicated *Hotel Terminus* to Mrs. Bauteaux, a good neighbor. If I were coming from a religious perspective, the act Mrs. Bauteaux attempted was a greater act of worship, respect, and understanding of God than any of the trappings of her life. That is how people need to judge each other. Will you risk your own life to save someone in danger?"

It is ironic that David ended our conversation with the story of a good neighbor. We met so he could vent his frustration about Christian zealots who scream their message through bullhorns during Mardi Gras festivities. While their methods may be offensive, they have the same spirit of Mrs. Bauteaux in *Hotel Terminus*: they truly believe they are snatching people away from danger.

I sat in silence as David put his phone in his pocket, discarded his coffee cup, and walked out the door. Clearly, he embraces the gospel of the God he doesn't believe exists. Jesus not only risked his life, he sacrificed his life to save humanity from danger. David has not rejected God, but, in his words, the "human trappings" people in the church add. He is a true son of Adam listening to serpents and making judgments before the one judged faces his accusers.

If I embraced David's atheism, my rock would be no greater than the creations of unreliable humans who cannot save themselves from death. I pondered David's rock, and then I thought, *Yeah, right*. It sounded like so much nonsense to me.

Conclusion

The Bible defines God's character, love, as one who is not proud and boastful. Content to labor unseen by human eyes, he seldom draws attention to himself. Just as the wind is unseen but observed by the swaying of flowers in a gentle breeze, we see God in the results of his actions. As I listened closely to the storyteller, I often perceived things the teller had missed. More than once, I opened an e-mail message and read, "The story you wrote about me brought me to tears."

While it was not my intent to answer an atheist challenge to "tell me what God is doing today," when I started writing these stories, that is what this book became. "I'm not writing about you," I told people who shared their stories with me. "Discovering what God has done in your life is my purpose." That quest has led me on a journey with no end in sight.

The Apostle John surmised "if everything Jesus did were written down the world would not have room for the books that would be written" (John 21:25). At this point in time, I doubt the universe could contain the books that could be written about God's continuing actions.

To the best of my ability, I recorded each person's story with impartiality. I pray their stories have inspired, encouraged, and challenged you to reach for the one who "is not far from each one of us" (Acts 17:27).

About the Author

Teena Myers is a freelance writer; editor of NOLA.com's Faith, Beliefs, and Spirituality blog; certified Belief Therapist; member of the Southern Christian Writers Guild and The Northshore Literary Society. She worked in Children's ministry, Christian television and taught Sunday School before she found her God given niche of writing. Teena lives on the west bank of New Orleans with Rod, her husband of twenty-seven years, who has ministered to children for thirty years. They have two sons, Seth and Timothy. Seth and his wife, Tina, have blessed them with three grandchildren.

To learn more about Teena, visit teenalmyers.com, friend Teena on Facebook (www.facebook.com/teena.myers), or email her teenamyers@ymail.com.